Also by Sinéad Murphy:

Effective History

The Art Kettle

Zombie University

Pandemic Response and the Cost of Lockdowns
(Co-edited with Aleida Mendes, Yossi Nehushtan
and Peter Sutoris)

Autistic Society Disorder

Sinéad Murphy

ISBN 978-1-4457-6258-6

Printed and bound by Lulu Press, UK

Contents

And Finished knowing – then –

Emily Dickinson

Preface

In 2018, one in one hundred British children was diagnosed with Autistic Spectrum Disorder. In the US, the number was even higher: one in fifty-nine American children was that year diagnosed with ASD.

There is speculation as to what may account for this growing phenomenon. There is suspicion of vaccination programmes. There is consideration of genetic links and environmental factors. There is acknowledgment of the broadening of the definition of autism and of improved diagnostic procedures. There are claims about our better understanding of the condition.

What is not heard is that the increasing autism *in* our society is directly linked to the increasing autism *of* our society. Our problem is not only that society is forced to designate more and more of its children as autistic, but that society is itself autistic, defined by the disorder it is so ready to diagnose.

Autism is not an easy condition to specify, characterised as it is by an array of diverse symptoms that vary dramatically in their severity. Nonetheless, all diagnoses of autism rely at least upon observation of the following: blockages to meaningful interaction and rigidity in patterns of thought and behaviour. These are the classic symptoms of autism. And these are the classic symptoms of our society.

The citizens of our autistic society receive many different diagnoses than that of autism. Anxiety and depression, for example, are rife, as are the drugs that are used to administer them. But among these various conditions, autism occupies a particular and significant place: because of its ambiguous straddling of institutions of health, education and care; because of the apparent unpredictability of its outcomes; because it manifests itself at an early age though not at birth; because of its almost infinitely accommodating 'spectrum'; and, most of all, because it mirrors, in each individual it seeks to manage, the symptoms of a society that is so very prone to managing – diagnoses of autism work to conceal the inhumanity of a society in which even the very young are unable to feel at home.

The child with autism is best understood as issuing a first-order rejection of the autism of our society, against which many of the other impairments to our health and happiness constitute less direct and immediate rejections. She cries out, in effect, on behalf of us all, against a society that is bad for us all and going to great lengths to suppress those who sense that that is so.

Thankfully, it is not easy to suppress a child with autism. Still, she will shriek in distress and delight. Still, she will spin and flap and bolt for the border at any chance she can get. Still, she will be heard above the heavy traffic of techniques being brought to bear on her.

What she demands is the restoration of precisely those horizons of living, learning and loving that our society's institutions have surely erased.

Whether we can respond to her demands – whether we can re-enter into the meaningful forms of life that she so craves – is not certain. What is certain is that more and more of our children are willing us to try.

1

Beginning

My little boy, Joseph, began life as a miscarriage. Between the fifth and eighth weeks of his gestation, there was heavy bleeding and the doctor advised that the pregnancy had ended. An internal scan at eight weeks showed unexpectedly that the pregnancy continued. And it did continue, though with anomalies that began to appear at about twenty weeks and that never receded until the end. The bump was small. Joseph's limbs were short. His weight was not what it should be. It was decided that birth would be induced at thirty-seven weeks, at which point Joseph should be able to suck milk and might do better outside of the womb, in which he did not appear to be thriving.

At thirty-five weeks, I got up one night to use the bathroom. Blood came gushing onto the floor. Wrapping a towel around me, I walked back to bed and rang for an ambulance. We lived about eight-hundred yards from the region's emergency hospital, so, within a couple of minutes, a paramedic was in the room. Having asked a few questions, he inserted a canula in my arm, which I later learned was intended to prepare for a blood transfusion. When the ambulance arrived, the first paramedic left. I was helped downstairs and into the van. The drive to the hospital took about two minutes, during which the second paramedics made a derisory comment about the first paramedic for his having, unnecessarily as they appeared to judge it, put the needle in my arm.

The delivery ward was ready. I was placed on a bed with the back raised. Staff explained that I was to have a caesarean section. When they tried to examine me, I started to cry. They seemed confused and kindly asked me what was wrong. I did not know what to tell them. I was wheeled into the operating theatre, where I was introduced to the anaesthetist and supported into a sitting position to receive an epidural. The anaesthetist was at one side of me; a senior midwife was at the other. They were listening at my back or my belly. The anaesthetist looked at the midwife – *That's mum's heartbeat, isn't it?* The midwife looked back – *That's baby's.* Everyone began to do things very quickly. I was helped to lie back, a mask was placed over my mouth and nose, and that was it.

I had had a placental abruption. Joseph was becoming distressed and I had lost a lot of blood.

The next thing I knew was the feeling of choking. Looking vaguely to my left, I saw a small baby in a glass cot, tiny and with a tube in his nose. His cheekbones were prominent; he was thin. He had arrived into the world crying loudly, which had made everyone there feel immediately relieved. Joseph was fine.

Until, three years later, he was diagnosed with autism.

*

I do not know whether the conditions of Joseph's pre-natal existence, or the trauma of his birth, are the cause of Joseph's autism. Studies have certainly been done, which appear to show a link between premature birth and diagnoses of ASD. But the link is still a tenuous one, and it is not the connection that I see between the circumstances of Joseph's first phase of life and Joseph's autism.

What strikes me now about the events that led up to Joseph's birth was made salient to me a day or two after we returned home from hospital. Throughout the pregnancy, there had been no continuity of midwife provision; I saw a different midwife almost every time I went for a check-up. But the first visit when we were back at home was from a midwife in her early sixties, to whom I told the details of Joseph's story. I say 'story' now, but it was not until that midwife casually remarked, *It's all connected of course*, that I considered that the early almost-miscarriage, the second and third trimester anomalies, and the eventual abruption were part of a single narrative.

Even to a non-professional, this narrative does make sense. Persistent heavy bleeding in early pregnancy must surely deplete the gestation environment. In such an environment, a baby might not get enough food and so might prioritise growing organs over growing limbs. And such an environment might be likely to collapse altogether in the end, to detach from its support system and finish the bleeding-out that it had begun with.

All of this makes common sense. All of this seemed to make medical sense to the midwife in her sixties. But all of this had been missed by every one of the many professionals and screening systems that I had encountered during the previous seven months. It was unsettling to hear the midwife mention it so casually, as if the eventual abruption had been a slow-motion car-crash, unfolding before everyone's eyes without anyone attending to it. It seemed outrageous, that no one had thought even to begin to notice it, that no one had communicated any detail of Joseph's history to anyone else, that no one had joined the dots, that a rigid adherence to measurements and procedures instead had ruled the day.

Poor communication and rigidity of thought and action are the classic symptoms of autism. The autism of the health service had prevented Joseph and me from being attended to appropriately.

Did the autism of the health service cause Joseph's autism? That is not what I wish to say – whether a baby born after an abruption is more or less likely to later be diagnosed as autistic, I do not know. What I do know is that an autistic health service, allied with an autistic education service and an autistic care service, is part of an autistic society in which inadequately meaningful interactions and rigidity of thinking and behaving are producing an ever-expanding remainder, a growing cohort of children who are unable to fit in as they are expected to do.

It is a common assumption, that there has always been autism but that only now, in our enlightened milieu, is it appropriately allowed for and understood. I do not share this common assumption. There has not always been autism. There have always been shy people, awkward people, retiring people, withdrawn people, of course. But, before the twentieth century, there were no autistic people – autism did not exist.

Do I mean that there is no such thing as autism? That autism is an illusion? Certainly not. Anyone who lives every day with the unrelenting, energy-sapping drip of demands placed upon them by an autistic child knows that autism is real. But knowing that autism is real is not the end of the story. Realities arise. They do not always have to have been there.

We are accustomed to this idea – that realities arise – when it comes to realities described by the biochemical sciences. We are accustomed to the fact that certain illnesses did not exist until certain poisons began to be added to the atmosphere, or certain mutations occurred in our genes. What we are less accustomed to is the fact that social, political and economic causes can produce realities, that concretely manifesting conditions, such as autism, can be caused, not only by the introduction of certain biology-altering ingredients (such as, I presume, are thought by some to be contained in the MMR vaccine) but by a set of experience-altering circumstances in the social, political and economic realms.

This book's central claim is that autism is a disorder of our society, and that one of its effects is to produce a set of children who, in mirroring this disorder, issue an unmanageable criticism of our society and suggest the mode of its redress.

I say that autistic children are *one* of the effects of Autistic Society Disorder. There are, inevitably, many others. The disorder is felt not only by those who find themselves in the grip of conditions such as anxiety and depression, but also by those who live what counts for a normal existence. Autistic Society Disorder is a condition that affects us all; those with a diagnosis of autism do no more, and no less, than call our attention to the condition and to the possibility of its cure.

How much longer they will continue to do this is uncertain. A meta-analysis of studies of trends in the diagnosis of autism, conducted by the University of Montreal and published in 2019, concluded that, in less than ten years' time, there will be no objective means of distinguishing between those in the population who merit the label 'autistic' and those in the population who do not. Time is not on our side. The autism of our society may be set to become so intense and so entrenched that every child will soon merit the label that is at present applied only to a percentage of children. In ten years' time, these children may not stand out as they do now. In ten years' time, their cries of distress may be lost in a general clamour whose lessons no one may remain to discern.

One last qualifier: I write always of the autistic *child* and not of autistic people generally. Yet, autistic children grow up, and many diagnoses of autism are given to adults. But there is something so startling and so pure about the autism of a child of five or six. Not because, at five or six, we are as nature would have had us; on the contrary, if autism is the social construct that I believe it to be, then a child with autism, no matter how young, is a social being. His startling purity lies simply in his undeveloped state, his inability, which he shares with all his very young peers, to be strategic, or cynical, to second-guess the process of his formation or to have it overlain by too many practices and categorizations for there to be the clarity that we need.

When a five-year-old covers her ears in the supermarket and spins and shouts out against the world, it is done in all the honesty of which we humans are capable. It is this autistic child to whom I appeal, as holding up the truest mirror, not to our nature but to our society.

Pillar Institutions

2

Health

In 1975, the World Health Organisation recorded its finding that the deprofessionalisation of primary health care was the single greatest requirement of its programme for improving worldwide health. Just short of half a century later, in March 2021, twenty-three world leaders, including the head of the World Health Organisation, agreed to the project of what they called 'One Health,' which is to institute the global advancement of the health and safety of 'all people, animals and the planet.' In 1975: an admission that our health is best tended outside of professional institutions. In 2021: a plan to escalate the professionalisation of health to new institutions with global reach.

It turns out that the great insight of the WHO, into the damaging consequences of relinquishing the ingredients of our health to the ministrations of health experts, never really caught on. On the contrary, since 1975, more and more of our capacity to experience and respond to changes in our own health has been outsourced to health institutions and, in the process, eroded beyond recall.

In this, the modern trajectory of health has shared in the modern trajectory of education and care. It has first been posited as an isolated and definable achievement, plucked out of the cut and thrust of life and delineated as a discrete phenomenon. Having been thus isolated and defined, it has been enshrined in institutions of health, to be known and improved in accordance with measurements and standards invented by those institutions and applied across the board to whole populations. Finally, having lost its vibrancy, having had the life sucked out of it, it has been returned to us, who, stripped of our capacities to experience it as a condition of individuals, can do nothing but continue the appeal to invented standards that is the only way for us now to be 'healthy.' Hence the ward-without-walls that, in our society, is coterminous with the classroom-without-walls and the home-without-walls in which we are now sequestered with small hope of release.

Within this trajectory of mortification-by-institution, the three themes – health, education, care – are nonetheless distinguishable; each has its own job to do, its own particular role in that dismantling of possibilities for meaningful interaction and lively thought and behaviour which constitutes Autistic Society Disorder. The job of health is quickly summarized: to constitute a *truth* that must be brought to light – *my health* – a truth that is accessible only to professionals and amenable only to pharmaceuticals, and that sets at naught everything that I might feel and understand as an embodied and embedded being. The job of health, in short, is to kill my body that feels.

*

The blockages to interaction that comprise one of the classic symptoms of autism most evidently prevent the autistic child from understanding and relating to other people. What is less evident is the impact on her ability to understand and relate to herself. The child with autism has sometimes profound difficulties with accessing how or what she feels. There is, for this reason, as significant an *intra*personal problem for the child with autism as there is the more widely broadcast *inter*personal problem. Her body seems not to be able to send her even those very basic messages that we expect to come naturally to us, messages of hunger, for example, or of pain. She appears not to have these sensations, or, if she does have them, not to understand what they mean.

Even at seven years old, Joseph has never yet seemed to feel hungry or full; he eats what he is given to eat, and that is all. Neither does he display conventional negotiations of pain; often he will worry at a cut or a graze so as to cause it to deteriorate and, presumably, to become more painful. He seems to be prevented in some manner from receiving meaningful communications from his insides. This typical aspect of being autistic is often summarised with reference to 'sensory processing'; autism seems to involve a scrambling of sensory information such that the child with autism is as much a stranger to herself as she is to the people around her. She really seems not to know how to feel.

As for why she does not know how to feel, this is a question currently without answer, filed with most of the other questions about autism, under 'Eventually To Be Given An Answer By The Health Sciences.' In the meantime, we shuffle along with the foreshadow of that answer, vaguely presuming that there's something somewhere in her brain, or something somewhere in her gut, or something somewhere in her brain-gut axis, in short, something somewhere *in her*. But what if the answer does not lie in her? What if the answer lies in her world, in our world? What if the child with autism cannot feel because conditions for feeling are on the wane? What if her inability to 'process' the information picked up by her senses is explained by there being increasingly very little for our senses to pick up? What if our society so systematically blocks the messages that we might receive from and through our bodies that none of us, by now, is good at knowing how to feel?

Perhaps this goes too far. Most of us, surely, do not have problems with sensory processing. Even very young children are good at knowing how they feel, reaching for the bread because they are hungry or looking to be embraced because they are in pain. The autistic child's difficulties with feeling must, after all, lie *in her*. But there is another possibility: that most of us, including most of our children, have learnt to submit to the abstract versions of feeling that are allowed to us in a society defined by its systematic assault upon real feeling; and that the autistic child's struggle with 'sensory processing' is one example of her extraordinary attunement to a society that is itself autistic.

Where might we look for this, our society's assault upon real feeling? In a rather unlikely place: in its meticulous attention to our health. Indeed, that which we call 'health,' an invention of the institutions of what we call our 'health service,' is nothing other than a wholesale offensive against our 'sensory processing,' a deliberate attack on our body that feels. And all our attending to our health, our looking after our health, our checking our health, our screening our health, are nothing else than our attending to a truth about us that we can never feel, our looking at a truth about us that we can never see, our checking the results of measurement procedures that disregard our senses, our screening ourselves from the insights of our bodies.

Health, in our autistic society, works to deaden our bodies, by systematically neglecting what our bodies might feel so that a truth of institutional invention is allowed to carry the day.

*

A common scenario:

You are invited by the UK's National Health Service to a free over-forties 'health check,' as part of an initiative that purports to aim at early identification and treatment of the most common health problems. The result is to be a healthier aging population, and a health service that is not clogged with patients whose sickness might have been relatively easily avoided. So you go to see your doctor, adding to the expanding number of people who submit themselves for medical attention even though they do not feel unwell, those women, for example, who for years have undergone screening for cervical and breast cancers. This is 'public health,' which addresses the health not of individuals but of populations, based on analyses of likelihoods distilled from the vast troughs of information to which governments and their institutions now have access. You go to see your doctor, not because you feel unwell, but because you are *a man in your forties*. Or rather, *you* don't go to see your doctor at all; *a man in his forties* goes to see his doctor.

And here is what happens when *a man in his forties* goes to see his doctor:

Firstly, he donates to the data bank, filling out a long form and providing the kind of information that his doctor might be thought already to be aware of. But this form is not for the doctor's information so much as it is for the system's perfection – and, though most of it is null and void, having already been incorporated into one of the system's algorithms, what is to be lost in spending half an hour in which some new information just might come to light? *A man in his forties* gives his pound, of data not of flesh, and waits for his turn to be seen.

Except that it never is his turn to be seen. Yes, his name appears on the waiting room's electronic display. Yes, he

walks to the indicated office. Yes, he enters and speaks to a woman with a stethoscope around her neck. And yes, she raises her head above her computer screen and looks at him right in the eyes. But still, it is never his turn to be seen. It is no longer the role of a doctor to see her patients. Her role, like the role of *a man in his forties*, is to service the health system, there being a layer of data which, for now at least, can only be mined by the professional application of electronic measuring instruments. Instead of seeing her patient, the doctor merely administers the instruments' endpoints, facilitating that body-contact without which the system's circuit is not complete.

Once the circuit is complete, once *a man in his forties* is fully hooked up, then the system really gets to work, extracting data from the innermost recesses of his body to perfect the algorithm, and inserting drugs to the innermost recesses of his body to perfect him. The remit of 'public health,' after all, is not to amass vast heaps of information but to sort those heaps and bring their findings to bear on the individual units that comprise the populations that are the target of 'public health' interventions. Having been wired in, *a man in his forties* is issued with prescriptions, for drugs that will normalise his measurements: taking the pills, he is promised, will alter his vital statistics according to 'public health' ideals, transforming him from *a man in his forties* to *Man In Forties*, straight off the health institution's assembly line, which is well oiled and highly productive.

Over thirty-five million adults in the US now take a medication known as 'Statins,' which operate on cholesterol levels to bring them in line with the norm; the National Institute for Health and Care Excellence in the UK published recommendations in 2014 which, if applied, would see almost all men over sixty taking the drug. *Man Over Sixty*, just like *Man In Forties:* another of the health institution's one-size-fits-all substitutes for the droves of real people who find themselves walking through its doors, replacing millions of human beings, born of women and formed by life, with millions of pharma beings, born of health abstractions and formed by health interventions.

Our health service is surely not in the business of seeing its patients. It is in the much bigger business of managing the population, distributing startling amounts of products of the pharmaceutical industry in response, not to how people are feeling, but to standards invented by itself and exported as ideal. The fact that approximation of these standards may reduce numbers of, say, strokes and heart-attacks is a much-appealed-to but somewhat moot point. At base, it is worth considering that average life expectancy in the UK and the US has not increased significantly in fifty years, and has indeed, for the first time since records were taken, recently begun to decrease. That death, now, is more likely to be a result of the side-effects of prescribed drugs than it is to be the final event in the progress of some disease may not be what we might wish to consider as improvement in healthcare.

Now, it so happened that the data extracted from your body that day by the health institution's measuring instruments actually accorded with 'public health' recommendations. *A man in his forties*, in this instance, already was *Man In Forties*, without the intervention of the meds. You already were 'healthy.' But that did not suffice. The institution merely cast its net a little wider, doubling down on its demand for conformity. From one of your responses on the long form was extracted information that your grandmother suffered a stroke at fifty-nine and your father died of heart-disease at seventy-two. This information, about people other than you, added another layer to identification of risk, and so *a man in his forties* who was also already an ideal *Man In Forties* was, yes, prescribed Statins, to manage a cholesterol level that was not actually abnormal but deduced as likely to become so.

Thus the UK National Health Service, staffed by its professionals and oiled by its pharmaceuticals, attended that day to what is called 'your health,' by reading off a set of numbers emitted by electronic devices, numbers whose significance relies upon in-house designators, such as 'cholesterol level,' which none of us has any chance of actually feeling. In such a scenario, what does it matter, the state of your or your doctor's 'sensory processing'? You might as well both be autistic. In fact, you are both autistic, sufferers from Autistic Society Disorder, so incapable of meaningful interaction that you spend your time together by feeding data into a computer programme, and so rigid in your patterns of thought and behaviour that no detail about you as an actual person living in the world is allowed to impinge on the usual routine – the Statins are prescribed, no matter what.

Tell me, how do you feel? A most fundamental question, which used to open every doctor's visit. A most fundamental question, which would, in this scenario, have raised the curtain on the whole charade – if you recall, you were feeling fine.

But the charade is safe. Because your doctor is unlikely to ask the question – really to ask it, that is, prepared really to respond to the reply. And why would she ask it? After all, it was not you who went to your doctor. It was *a man in his forties.* And you know very little about *a man in his forties*, certainly nothing of how such a being is supposed to feel. Even less, of course, do you know anything about *Man In Forties*, 'healthy' you, that entirely abstract creature for whom mere human feelings are beside the point. 'Healthy' you is a system being, a data being, a phantasm of 'public health' initiatives, and you, or I, or any of us, has no idea at all how it is feeling or what might be good for it.

*

But if *you* did not go to the doctor that day, where did you go? If flesh-and-blood you was not the being hooked up to the health system's circuit, then were you left behind somewhere, untouched by the institution's instruments, lying dormant, ready to reassert yourself at some future time, ready to attend once more to how you really feel and to insist that your doctor does the same? The answer to this question reveals the sinister extent of Autistic Society Disorder.

When the metal endpoint of the health institution's measuring instrument touches our skin, there is an important ambiguity about what it is there to do. Explicitly, it is there to determine the state of our health, to check our health. But what is our health? It is not, as we have seen, significantly related to how we feel. It is something quite different, something that we cannot feel, something that is a mystery to us, to be discovered only by the instruments and the abstract categories they serve. The instruments are there, then, to divine a *truth* about us – our health status – of which we would otherwise be ignorant, to unearth a state of affairs that lies so deeply encrypted in our body that we cannot experience it or testify to it but that nonetheless defines us, tells the truth about us, in ways that nothing more manifest can achieve.

And yet, for all that our health, which the instruments are there to discover, is that most true of truths about us, which lies so deep within us that we cannot ourselves experience it, the objects that the health institution's instruments seek to measure (cholesterol, for example), the units of those objects' measurement (mg per dL of blood, for example), and the standards of normal and abnormal against which those measurements are judged (70-130 mg/dL, for example) are not at all about any particular one of us, but apply across the board and without discrimination (to every *man in his forties*, for example).

In being directed towards a truth about you, which runs so deeply that you cannot feel it, the instruments and their categories and products are simultaneously directed towards a truth about a huge, generic group, which applies so generally that you cannot feel it. It is this conflation, of the discrete individual (your health) and generic diagnoses and prescriptions (health standards and products) that is defining of 'public health,' which decommissions anything that we might possibly experience, anything that we might actually feel. Flesh-and-blood is dissolved by 'public health' and its essentially ambiguous appeal to a vital truth that is at once too personal and too general for us to feel.

We may begin now to appreciate the effect of all that attention that we pay to our health, which works, not to make us feel better but to stop us from feeling at all. Given that, to us non-professionals, our health is nothing but that which we cannot feel, our efforts to look after our health can consist of nothing but our active neglect of what we feel. And what is the upshot of this neglect? What is the fate of flesh-and-blood you, when all that you can do in the effort to attend to your health is to refuse to take seriously what your flesh and blood might tell you? We make a grave mistake if we imagine that, being of flesh and blood, you sit solidly in the wings, waiting to spring into action when you are wanted once more. No. The moment that you take those Statins – well before that moment actually, the moment that you respond to the health service's call, not to you but to *a man in his forties* – you submit to being remade, from the inside out, as a being alien to yourself, so unaccustomed to consulting your own body that the messages that it might send you are blocked.

In our system of autistic health, it is not only that we cease to trust what our bodies tell us; our bodies stop telling us. Knowing how to feel does not keep in the absence of being practiced. Like a limb that lies unmoved, it atrophies from neglect, and wastes away.

It is true, a central effect of our health system is to persuade us that this cannot happen, that intrapersonal experiences are immune to being blocked, that nothing can make us a stranger to our own body. These experiences are advertised to us as basic, intuitive, only-you-can-tell. And the instruments that are applied to measure them are advertised as neutral, as dead metal hooked up to servile programmes, only recording what is *there*. But the very concept of the intrapersonal, established as it is as distinct from the interpersonal, is a distraction. There is no aspect of my experience that is beyond being worked on, altered, managed. What we regard as the intrapersonal is as interpersonal an achievement as any. Or, in other words, my knowing how to feel – pain, or hunger, for example – is not *my* knowing how to feel but *our* knowing how to feel: a shared, mutually supported accomplishment that is meaningful and ritualized.

Flesh-and-blood is a cultural phenomenon, after all – shaped in complex ways to send us messages that we learn to attend to and understand. In our society, we are told that these messages are 'natural,' that there is no learning required to attend to and understand them. Persuaded that they are 'natural,' we have then no grounds for suspecting that they might be blocked, that we might unlearn the ability to attend to and understand them, that we might relinquish this possibility, outsource it, to the abstractions of the health institution with its professional procedures and products. And yet, this outsourcing of our capacity to feel our own bodies is precisely what occurs in Autistic Society Disorder. Culturally shaped experiences of our bodies are trumped by the outputs of medical circuitry; ritualized, traditional formation of our bodies is replaced by the insertion of pills; and flesh-and-blood at last is heard of no more. In the end, we forget how to feel, forget how to experience our bodies in any way other than via abstract measurements applied to by professionals. Our bodies lose their vitality, under the careful ministrations of institutions of health.

*

Perhaps it may be considered that all of the above began with a 'health check,' and that a health check is not typical of our interaction with our own bodies and with the institutions of health; that we mostly go to see the doctor, for instance, because we are feeling unwell, in which case we certainly do know how we feel and are listened to by our doctor as we recount it. But is this really so? Or do we now do a 'health check' even as we go through the motions of attending to how we feel?

Say that I develop a pain in my face and jaw on the left side. It doesn't seem to be a problem with a particular tooth. It comes in waves and subsides for periods of up to an hour. What do I do? I do a health check, of course. I look up my symptoms online. The results are alarming: possible aneurism, auto-immune disease, absyss, facial neuralgia. I speak to my mother; she suggests, of her own accord, that it might be facial neuralgia. *Yes!*, I reply, *I read about that*. I am strangely settled by the second opinion, somehow comforted by the clinical atmosphere of our joint diagnosis.

But why? Why am I thus consoled? Why do I have the sense of something being resolved, of a truth being uncovered, by the term 'facial neuralgia'? What *is* facial neuralgia? When I look up that online, the first answer is that facial neuralgia involves sharp, intermittent pain in the face and jaw – I did not need to be told about that. All other answers contain references to body parts (the trigeminal nerve) and diseases (multiple sclerosis) which are far removed from my capacity to interact with, being objects for medical professionals. And yet, I experience the truth about my situation in an abstract categorisation made available by the health institution rather than in the pain in my face with which I began, and which, if I attended to in the context of having a practiced intelligence at attending to my body – in the context of actually knowing how to feel – I might understand in a meaningful manner: Is it the result of sitting or lying in a draught, made pernicious by a change in wind direction? Why does it extend to just below my eye when the discomfort I experienced last November was centred solely around my jaw? And so on.

It turned out that the pain in my face and jaw was, according to my dentist, the result of my doing what she reported many of her clients are also doing: grinding my teeth in my sleep, caused, so she said, by 'anxiety.' *Anxiety!* I thought, leaping at the consolation of another abstract health category. But the rot had to stop there. Much and all as I thrilled with relief at the offer of another of the health institutions' labels – the UK National Health Service now even describes and diagnoses what it calls the 'specific condition' of Generalised Anxiety Disorder – I strained to resist its promise of comfort. I was not suffering from 'anxiety.'

Rather, my whole body was tense with neglect, and strained from the effort of interaction with myself and others through the prism of generic categorisations that do not map on to anything that I might feel. The little tremor of salvation I experienced at the news that my teeth grinding is a condition known as 'bruxism' was like the death rattle of a body grown sick and tired of being systematically ignored.

Another health check, then, though without the official health check credentials. Another instance of the overriding of anything that we might feel by the experience of having learnt the truth, of having found out *what's really wrong with me*. Yes, the forms of feeling were still in play; vestiges of meaningful interaction, still abroad. I spoke to my mother, who listened to my complaints. I walked out into the world and met a dentist, just as, even for the official health check, you walked out into the world and met a doctor. But these rudimentary interactions are fast going out of style. The technology is in place to obviate them almost entirely.

The UK NHS has long encouraged its patients to avail themselves of its phone provision of professional advice and assistance. Insurance companies are making body technologies available to clients to 'help' them to reduce insurance payments as a reward for 'healthy' life choices. And at the official health check, you were offered a device to bring home, which monitors and records your blood-pressure over the course of a day. How long before the device is strapped on to your body for most of the time? Inserted into your body, perhaps? And how long before it not only monitors and records, but also administers the drugs? The technology is getting there; it is only a matter of introducing it in a manner not to disturb a population about to be entirely hooked up.

New regulations in the UK allow pharmacists to sell Statins without a doctor's prescription; a lay-over, we might presume, to their administration by some proxy pump, strapped onto us, or into us, for life. Like a parent tiptoeing out of the room, still singing softly to their sleeping child, our health institutions are gradually withdrawing, still looking into our eyes and speaking to us in soothing tones, lest we come to and find that we cannot feel.

In the meantime, the abstractions accumulate, though the taxonomies begin to grow lazy, the labels more cartoonish – 'Generalised Anxiety Disorder' is not a sophisticated designator; even less so, among doctors in a deprived part of England, is the recently diagnosed condition of 'Shit Life Syndrome.'

*

But my example may still be skewed. After all, I did look up my pain online, and so conducted a health check, albeit unofficial, submitting myself to the deadening effect of professional labelling when I might instead have attended to my body's messaging, when I might instead

have felt my pain. Would this have trumped the health-check mode? Would this have been a readmission of the body that feels? Perhaps not. For, it may be that the experience of bodily discomfort as 'pain' is itself a crude labelling in the health check mode, skimming over any delicate interaction with our body with the go-to health label par excellence, the label of all others that consigns our body to obscurity. The body experienced as in pain is the body already half-dead.

In his book *Limits to Medicine*, Ivan Illich observes that most Indo-Germanic languages have a plethora of terms which are translated with our catch-all 'pain.' There are 'hard work,' 'toil,' 'trial'; there are 'torture,' 'endurance,' 'punishment'; there are 'affliction,' 'illness,' 'tiredness,' 'hunger,' 'mourning,' 'injury,' 'distress,' 'sadness,' 'trouble,' 'confusion,' 'oppression'; and many other descriptors, some of which are used by us but not with the resonance of our umbrella term 'pain,' into which we increasingly place all negative experiences, be they physiological, psychological, social, financial, spiritual, or otherwise. Grief at the loss of a close relative is officially allowed, by the DVA handbook, to be grief for only three days, after which it is redefined merely as pain…

…and pain, of course, must of be relieved. It will come as no surprise that, to help with the pain in my face, I had taken paracetamol, as I do for all pain. This has the effect of exempting me from a whole range of discomforts which I have, in consequence, no practice at discriminating between, for which I have only that bald term 'pain' and which I have no experience of enduring. I had taken a painkiller and had therefore, quite explicitly and deliberately, silenced even the crude message that my body was sending. I had killed my pain, and with it the last fibre of my body that feels.

I am not alone. A University of Oxford study in 2016 showed that UK citizens consume over six thousand tonnes of paracetamol every year, an average of seventy tablets each. And the Consumer Health Products Association in the US estimates that each week twenty-three percent of American adults make use of the drug. The numbers are staggering, but they are news to no one for whom half-used blister packs of the product are a common sight, slipping out of trouser pockets and spilling out of handbags. We reach for a pill to block the messages being sent to us by our own faltering bodies, often more than daily.

And it is never too young to begin. The pharmaceutical wing of our institutions of health have ensured that paracetamol is 'safe' for the very young, suspended in a saccharine syrup. Twelve million bottles of the most popular brand of this sweet soother are sold every year in the UK, where the medicines regulator estimates that eighty-four percent of children are given the drug before they are weaned. Too soon to take anything more than their mother's milk (likely to contain paracetamol anyway, given that it is 'safe' to take when breastfeeding), the process begins of deadening little bodies that have only just come to life.

*

But our paracetamol habit may be only the gateway. For, there is a more profound deadening now sweeping our society, in which it is so anathema to receive messages from our bodies that embodiment itself has become objectionable, in which we are so at a loss about how to feel that only a wholesale suppression of feeling is bearable, in which we are so incapable of processing the stimulation of our senses that our senses must be dulled at any cost.

In 2017, more Americans died of an opioid overdose than died in the whole of the Vietnam War. In the same year, the UK NHS issued twenty-four million prescriptions for the drugs, double the number issued fifteen years before. The demand is now overwhelming, for products to numb our bodies whose very existence can be experienced as nothing more nuanced, nothing more sufferable, nothing more meaningful, than pain. And pain is the biggest outrage of all.

The ambiguity that defines 'public health' is tightening its stranglehold at last: on the one hand, the pain you feel is your pain and only yours, an anomaly so deep inside of you that it makes no sense to try to attend to it or understand it without specialist assistance; on the other hand, this specialist assistance comes in a one-size-fits-all pill, rolled out across the population at large. Bewildered by this sleight of hand, which conflates the deepest truth about us with the most widespread characteristics of humankind; rendered doubly passive in respect of a state of affairs that is so personal and so impersonal that it is, on both fronts, beyond us; bereft of contexts of meaning with which to relativise and thereby suffer sensations that are therefore unbearable: there is nothing for us to do with our bodies but numb them. So prone now to reaching for whatever abstract label will explain us, we are ready recipients of whatever distilled substance will cure us. The institution of health: now a one-stop-shop in which even the category *Man In Forties* seems like a hand-crafted specifier; a production line for the manufacture of only one type of being: a zombie, nodding out, a walking dead.

The 'opioid epidemic' has been in the media as a 'public health crisis.' It is not. It is a public health climax. It is the institution of health playing out its endgame, writing the final chapter of a society in which we cannot interact, even with ourselves, except through the mediation of abstract labels and their associated products, and in which patterns of thought and behaviour have grown so rigid that they are all of them called simply 'pain' and all of them treated the same.

This health climax is also a health culmination: the 'opioid epidemic' brings to fruition the Autistic Society Disorder from which it also offers a final escape, pharmaceutically engineering that disassociation from embodiment that other aspects of the health institutions' engineering have produced more elaborately and invisibly.

How does an opioid work to kill your pain? It does not diminish your pain so much as dull your capacity to feel it. When you use opioids, you know that there is pain but, somehow, it does not seem like yours. The perfect pharmaceutical culmination of a disorder that has remade a population to be unable to feel: scrambled by a two-prong assault, from the abstractions of our health institutions and from the drugs that do the rest of their work; and reconstituted as sites for the implantation of statistics and side-effects which are the new, autistic version of human ailment, autistic because they do not arise as part of a holistic pattern of embodiment and autistic because they are treated to the same blanket cure every time.

During the birth of my older boy, one of the midwives who attended began to ask me whether I wanted to push. I could only answer that I did not know. Quite a surprise. You would think that you would know how to feel whether a baby inside your body was intent on getting out. You would think that nobody would know better than you. You would think that this would be an intuitive matter, a question of basic, intrapersonal messaging. But that was not so. Having never felt such a thing before, and living as I do in a society in which others' experiences of feeling it do not circulate, I did not, I could not, judge what was happening. I simply did not know how to feel. All I could do was experience pain – an utterly meaningless, and therefore utterly insufferable, pain.

One hears whispers – not much more – of the pain of childbirth. No doubt it has never been easy. But clearly it has not always been insufferable. In the appropriate context, under the supervision of those with whom one has a relationship or in whom one trusts, in the company of others who have been there before, the difficulty of childbirth has been bearable, has been borne. And indeed, even in the clinically abstract environment of the hospital delivery ward, and even in the company of a midwife I had never met before, even I managed to bear the journey to full dilation. But then, five hours in, the midwife I had never met before but in whom I had placed my trust – her name, I remember, was Emma – had to leave. Her shift was over. Institutional routines intervened in what, even under institutional conditions, had become a somewhat meaningful interaction: she, offering the right kind of encouragement; I, responding with confidence in her judgement. Another midwife arrived of course, although, in the hours that followed, she was replaced intermittently. But the spell had been broken. Exhausted and without my mentor, I could not begin to build up a trust in someone new. Almost immediately, the pain became unbearable. I asked for relief. Diamorphine was injected into my thigh. And I felt nothing more. The pain did not go away – I knew I was in pain. But it was no longer mine. I could not feel it. I could not care about it. Unfortunately, when my little baby made his appearance in the world, I could not care about him either. *Well, is it a boy or a girl?* the midwife prompted, encouraging me to attend to him. But, dead to all the world, I could only shrug with indifference.

And it is this indifference, this numbed, this muted, relation to what is going on about us and inside us that is abroad in our society, hanging in the air like an atmosphere that we must try very hard not to breathe. Between the professional labels to which we incessantly apply and the pharmaceutical products that buttress their effect, and with a vague conviction that both are connected to a truth about us and each other to which we would otherwise not gain access, it is ever more difficult for us to discern, to judge, to care, to really feel.

*

The question to which all of this leads:

If we sufferers from Autistic Society Disorder – we who have forgotten how to feel; we who are blocked from meaningful interaction even with ourselves and who are rigid to the point of having recourse to only a very few descriptions and only a very few prescriptions to experience what might otherwise be a rich and complex human existence – if we are all autistic, then who are those among us who receive the diagnosis? What makes you stand out as autistic in an autistic society?

Whatever the answer to this question, whatever it is in an autistic society that merits the diagnosis of autism, it has the effect of submitting you to the most wily label of them all, a label made available like all of its kind by the professionals that staff our institutions of health but that is so blatantly removed from anything that one might feel that, once assigned by those professionals, it is immediately declared as not a health matter at all. What this means is that a diagnosis of autism carries with it the promise that all such diagnoses carry: the promise of a truth, lying deep within, which is revealed by, and only by, the abstract labels of the health sciences – *Ah, I see, he's autistic.* And yet, the moment that the health institution delivers this truth – which has the effect of setting at naught what might otherwise be concrete and negotiable experiences of ourselves and others, as revealed by interactions with ourselves and others that are meaningful to us and not only to health professionals – it washes its hands of it, readily accepting that autism is not a health problem at all. It can be accompanied by health problems – severe constipation, for example – but in and of itself it has nothing to do with our health.

The autistic child, then, falls victim to the greatest sleight of hand of them all, made subject to the abstraction-effect of the institutions of health with which it has nothing else to do. In other words, a diagnosis of autism is nothing other than the putting beyond our grasp, as 'symptoms,' kinds of understanding and behaviour that we might otherwise find more fulsomely meaningful; the linking of styles of thought and action which we might otherwise interpret and interact with inventively with a truth of the health variety with which we have, of necessity, nothing much to do. Autism is in this respect the purest health condition of them all, consisting of nothing more than the add-on of meaningless truth with which the institution of health effaces our capacities for meaningful experience.

Not only this: having been made subject to the purest of all the health labels, the autistic child, as she grows older, is much more likely than her peers to find herself labelled with many more, less pristine, designators: anxiety, depression, Addictive Personality Disorder, Obsessive Compulsive Disorder, Generalized Anxiety Disorder, perhaps even Shit Life Syndrome. Children who receive a diagnosis of autism are four times more likely than those who do not to subsequently receive a diagnosis of depression, twelve times more likely than those who do not to be admitted to psychiatric institutions, and fifteen times more likely than their non-autistic peers to try to end it all in suicide.

And for what? What is it that, before this management by abstractions, causes a child in an autistic society to be labelled 'autistic'? It is something that is never considered, something quite wonderfully uplifting. It is their refusal of autism; their refusal of the encroaching meaninglessness of our inter, and intra, actions; their refusal of the rigidity of our hyper-normalised thoughts and behaviours; their insurmountable sense that the existence to which we are consigned, clogged as it by abstractions with which we can have nothing to do, simply will not suffice. The child with autism seems so often lost in a kind of vagueness – uninterested, unstimulated. She does not reach for the dog to stroke its fur, nor for the toy to hold its smooth wooden handle; she does not laugh at the antics of other children nor turn her head when someone calls her name. And then she is sometimes so absorbed, so over-stimulated, by things that we hardly see or hear at all, by the postcard that no longer lies idly on the mantelpiece or by the crying of a baby in a crowd. She is out of sync with what passes for the world around her, unmoved by what counts as meaning in her midst, left cold by cold abstractions, just as we all ought to be and really are in the end. As such, the child who is labelled 'autistic' might, if we could only allow it, be the best, the truest, litmus test of all, for the retreat of a world that has become to us so meaningless that none of us are really taken in by it anymore.

If we could only allow it...

Joseph was three years and three months old when, one Monday morning, I searched online for 'autism.' He had not yet begun to speak, but we felt relaxed about that. He was so clearly bright, and interested in things that he was interested in, and, although intermittently fractious, so generally content. But recently, coinciding with his toilet training, which we began when he turned three, he was becoming unusually distressed. He had seemed on two occasions to lose consciousness with distress, although he had come around so quickly and so easily that I could not trust that it had happened at all. Sometimes, I would summarise Joseph to those who asked about him, by carelessly remarking that, if we consulted a doctor, they'd be sure to label him 'autistic.' And then, one morning without any clear purpose, I searched for 'autism.' On the screen before me appeared a list of symptoms. Things that I would never have thought of as a symptom where there: walking on tiptoes, sniffing at things, spinning around. The more fundamental characteristics too, of course: lack of communication; uneven attention; tendency to extreme distress. I read through the list. And I felt a dawning. Not of a bright new day. But of a truth, even if the truth was dark. Joseph was autistic. *That's what's really wrong with him.*

Like all of the institution's labels, it took a load off. Like the opiates that do their work, it brought relief. But at what expense? The next weeks were a period of dreadful disaffection. Every time I thought of Joseph, every time I spoke to him or helped him, there was a great remove: *What he did there, was that Joseph or was that autism?* Between me and the little boy who was born so very small and who I had tended for three years and more, there had inserted itself, quickly and completely, a new and abstract category carrying with it a kind of truth that jostled for space with everything that I had learnt how to feel, blocking interactions that had been effortlessly meaningful, natural, making almost everything that I did and thought more careful, more deliberate, more rigid. That truth is jostling even now, always there with a comforting answer, an established programme, a prediction to rely upon and, yes, if I want them, an array of pills that will 'help.' To keep my hold of Joseph though it all, to not fall victim to Autistic Society Disorder in this, the eye of its storm, has been the biggest challenge of all the challenges presented by Joseph's autism.

Will Joseph keep hold of Joseph through it all? At a recent consultation in his school, the question was introduced – a question for the future, it is true – of when to tell Joseph that he is autistic. The rationale is not difficult to understand: to dispel Joseph's future confusion, at his failure to make friends or keep friends, for example, or at his feelings of anxiety in complex social settings. But still I shuddered at the prospect, of Joseph at last coming up for some air, of Joseph at last in a kind of clearing, of Joseph able to be told things about himself and the world, of his doing some wondering, perhaps, at himself and the world, of Joseph free, if only somewhat, from the heavy workload of manoeuvring himself in a world that is not made for him and his kind, of Joseph at last with just a little space to move about in: immediately suffocated by his diagnosis, immediately laden with a truth about himself to stifle any wondering at all. *Ah, I'm autistic, that's what really wrong with me.*

3

Education

What is it that has remade us for all of this? What has readied us to be hived off from our bodies, estranged from our senses, all the better to be submitted – and to submit ourselves – to the rule of labels and interventions devised, and endlessly revised, by institutions whose vested interests are increasingly explicitly at the helm?

What made you so willing to answer the health institution's call, to all *men in their forties*? What made you fall into step with the droves of those who are likewise following the call, going to the doctor and taking the drugs even though they do not feel unwell? What makes the doctor prescribe the drugs? What makes her so prone to playing out her medical ambitions – possibly spawned in an early hope of helping other people – at the keyboard of a massive computer, whose calculations she has no hope of ever comprehending but whose judgments she parrots in place of forming her own?

What has done this? What has come between me and my flesh and blood – between me and my little boy – that I must strive now to keep some hold upon him, upon my experience of him, upon a reality of him not entirely reconstituted by the parameters of his diagnosis?

What has done this? What has gained such traction that the moment that a child with autism clears a space to look about him, the moment that he is able to come to the surface for air, he is saddled with heaps of readymade content, plugged in to narrow and carefully managed tubes?

What has done this? What has so disenchanted all that might come to us through our bodies in the world, that a dependence upon invented labels and an obedience to constantly recalibrated programmes for their realisation have been so thoroughly implanted?

What has done this?

Education has done this. It is what education is for.

How has education done this? By teaching us, at every level of its institution and, as its institutions' walls gradually fall away, in every nook and cranny of life, one simple move: the step back, to take a better look.

*

Perhaps *the* classic symptom of the child with autism – more salient and widely discussed than his seeming not to know how to feel – is his distinctive and almost wholly predictable seeming not to know how to *look*. 'Eye contact' is a phrase with which anyone responsible for a child with autism is very familiar, because the child with autism will not make eye contact. Or not very often. Or not on the appropriate occasions.

I have argued that our knowing how to feel – pain, for example – is not the merely personal achievement that it is advertised as, but is social, worldly, all the way down. No need to repeat this argument now; no need to insist that knowing how to *look* is a social achievement, a worldly accomplishment. Knowing how to look, making 'eye contact,' actually underpins what counts for us as social connection and worldly involvement. Indeed, looking directly at someone or something is widely taken as evidence that we appreciate the significance of that someone or something. Even the human significance of that someone or something. Even the human significance of ourselves. Simon Schama, English historian and author of *The Face of Britain*, is surely not the only one to name the act of looking as the act that makes us human. Looking is – has become, at least – fundamental in our society, an essential criterion for full admittance to the club.

No surprise, then, that so much is made of the autistic child's indifference to looking; no surprise that it seems to justify the condition's very name. The child with autism, the child who will not look, is judged to be missing out, in a manner almost inhuman, on the full experience of other people and the world that we share with them. And so she is the object of a myriad interventions, with the aim of fostering in her that which it is judged ought to come quite naturally. *Good looking!* she is told, over and over again, when she gives a fleeting glance in the right direction.

Yet, there are anomalies in all of this, which mount up with the slightest analysis. One, particularly glaring: the child with autism is often unsettlingly insistent upon looking, staring and staring with startling intensity, until you join him in clapping hands, or show acknowledgment of his having finished the jigsaw, or respond to his request if he can make one, or because you are moving in a certain way or sitting in a certain attitude or wearing a certain kind of tie. And his looking is good looking. Only Joseph in our household will immediately notice that the tea towel on the cooker has been changed, and only Joseph will say *Wow!* when I appear downstairs in a new pair of trousers.

Another anomaly: those of us who are not autistic do not do as much looking as we might think. Anyone given the task of encouraging a child with autism to look may tell you that one of the real difficulties in the commission is to actually ourselves look in the eyes of the child we wish to help. How often we speak to people, while looking at something else or at nothing at all – we too, it turns out, are not so good at 'eye contact.' Even the everyday task of walking the city streets has become something of a challenge, as we weave our way through throngs whose eyes are not in contact with the pavement beneath them, nor in contact with the road beside them, nor in contact with the people around them, but at rest on some short text or tiny image shining at them from their phone. *Very good, sweetheart,* says the young mother in a strangely absent, wooden voice, repeating, as a reflex, that well-worn learned-off phrase, as she looks vacantly – autisticly? – at something other than her performing child, at a stream of high-definition stimuli too chaotic to be meaningful but distracting nonetheless.

And the biggest anomaly: this emphasis we place upon looking, which is, after all, the least impressive of our sensory achievements, conducted by the most lazy of our senses, the most passive, certainly when compared with the active incorporation of tasting, or the risky outreach of touch, or – greatest contrast of all – the federated awareness of equilibrium. When we look, our whole body can slump in its seat as we direct our eyes, half-lidded, at the world. When we look, it is our body that does it, but our body hardly awake, idling, almost insensible, its eye flitting from this to that or staring inertly and without purpose, so easily satisfied with summary content, with mere essentials, with a fly-over vista, with fly-by shots.

On that fateful Monday morning when I searched online for 'autism' and confronted a list of its symptoms, the infamous inability to make 'eye contact' was named first. But it was immediately followed by descriptions of hyper-abilities, all in the fields to which our other senses open: the autistic child sniffs, puts things in her mouth, flaps her hands, spins around, walks on tiptoes, and generally exhibits an aptitude for sensory experience that is much broader than the conventional, and intermittently much more joyful. Yet what is amplified is the autistic child's great disability: she does not look, not much at least, not as a matter of course as we do, not involuntarily, not passively. She does not rest her eyes as she is supposed to; she does not adopt that indifference that passes for us as 'eye contact'; she does not enter into that torpor of looking which is the final resting place of our bodies in our world.

How fitting it is, that 'to look' is one of those verbs in the English language that is most often employed in a phrasal variant; how appropriate, that we mostly look at, look over, look past, look through, look into and look up, all the while doing something far removed from sensibility. We look at an issue; we look over a file; we look past a mistake; we look through a document; we look into a case; we look up the meaning of a word; and have very little to do with what we actually see, preoccupied instead with what we think, with what we know, with what we can find out, in the *abstract*. Indeed, even when 'look' is abroad on its own, it has still often nothing to do with what is seen – *Look!* she says impatiently, determined that her interlocutor grasp the point of her argument.

Our looking, you see, draws us away from our eyes that can see, away from our body and its senses. When we look, we are, at best, passive recipients of vague and summary impressions, but, more usually, we are distilling the essential point, identifying the defining principle, seeking the theoretical implication, looking behind what presents to our senses for the general truth that we suspect them of hiding.

If this is so, it offers a much more fulsome explanation of children with autism than all of this truncated talk of 'eye-contact.' Because, if there is one thing to which children with autism are disinclined even more than they are disinclined to the listlessness of looking, it is to the cynicism of looking, of abstracting, of experiencing the particular as an instance of a general type, of acceding to some essential principle at stake in an experience or relation. Patrick is Patrick for many many years before he is ever 'my brother.'

And if this is so, it offers a much more fulsome explanation for the increase in numbers of children with autism than all of the loose talk of 'better awareness' and 'improved diagnostic procedures.' Because, if there is one milieu in which there would be an increase in numbers of children with autism, it is our society of looking, our society in which the eye has long been the Trojan horse for the encroachment of a general insensibility, a mania for the abstract, a growing disbelief in everything that is right before our eyes, our ears, our noses and tongues and nerves and guts, in favour of what is put into our heads: concepts, abstract concepts, which, together, amount to what we call 'knowledge,' that great gift to us all of our institutions of education.

*

In 1649, the Spanish painter, Diego Velasquez, produced a work entitled *Las Meninas*. In 1966, the French philosopher, Michel Foucault, wrote about it, as an early instance of a move that has defined our modern age. The painting is full of content and suffused with light and looking. But it is blighted on its left side by its depiction of the rear of an enormous painter's canvas, so enormous that one has the sense, in looking at *Las Meninas*, that one is looking at both of its sides, at the front with its colourful court scene and at the back, dull beige and braced with wood. In between, also portrayed in *Las Meninas*, is the painter, who has been working on the other side of the canvas whose rear side we are consigned to looking at, but who, if only for a moment perhaps, has stepped back from the canvas to take a better look: at his subject, at his painting….and at himself; the painter depicted in *Las Meninas*, brush poised above his palate, has been painted by the painter Diego Velasquez, brush poised above his palate. In *Las Meninas*, we encounter a clever and soon-to-be-characteristic move: the real-life Spanish painter painting himself painting, for which purpose the real-life Spanish painter steps back from himself painting, pauses in his painting, does something other than painting, looks at himself painting, looks from the outside of painting, looks behind the back of painting.

The effect of this clever move on the history of modern painting need not be dwelt upon; painting gradually came to be suspended, so that it might reflect upon itself, so that it might look at itself, so that it might paint painting. What else was Whistler doing when he allowed his canvas to go partly unpainted; what else was Van Gogh doing when he made his brush strokes salient; what else was Seurat doing when he showed the point of contact between his brush and his canvas; or Pollock with his splashes or Ryman with his smudges or Mondrian with his black lines or Malevich with his white squares? Each of them stepping back behind the last one, each of them moved to take a better look, to be the one really to have painted painting, really to have known what painting is and conceived of what painting must be. That a recent step back to take a better look at painting was an art installation in London, comprised of nothing more than the shutting down of the museum in which it was being exhibited, speaks volumes for the intimacy between getting a better look at painting and not doing any painting at all.

And as with painting so with everything, as our society has added to every possible skill, profession, hobby, to every involvement of every kind, a layer – accorded the most somber importance – of knowledge, of the theorising of those skills, professions, hobbies, involvements, of their conceptualisation. Like all our society's enterprises, this one too is subject to infinite growth, there being always another layer of looking, another step back to give that valued perspective on the last one.

You nurse, yes. But do you understand the ethics of your nursing decisions? But do you appreciate the role that ethical knowledge ought to play in the making of nursing decisions? In the education of nurses? Do you know the techniques that might be brought to bear on the education of nurses in the framing of their ethical knowledge and its relation to nursing decisions? Have you looked at the historical provenance of the techniques being brought to bear on the education of nurses in the framing of their ethical knowledge and its relation to nursing decisions…?

Layer after layer of analysis, each one seeking to shore up the last one, each one seeking to win, pressing pause on the previous, stepping back from it to take a better look, and filling the space that back-step opens up with newly mined or minted concepts, which grow ever less intuitively available to the non-expert and ever more fantastical.

How often we hear it now, from every side and through every medium: that we live in 'a knowledge society.' How much braying there is on the subject, as our 'knowledge society' is lauded, by our governments and their think-tanks, by our institutions and their managers. And by ourselves, who take knowledge to be a self-evident good, a no-brainer benefit, and who run ourselves and our children through the mill of those institutions that instill us with it, institutions that educate us so that those who end up doing – actually doing – some real nursing are ever more likely to never have been taught very much how to nurse and are woefully remunerated, and those who have been taught how to nurse have really been taught how to put nursing on pause, how to step back from nursing to take a better look at it…how to nurse remotely. The bigger the step back, the bigger the salary and the social eclat.

*

And we learn to step back now when we are very young.

When Joseph was five and in the second year of his compulsory schooling, the topic for one half-term was The Great Fire of London. An event from three hundred miles away and three hundred years ago. Our institutions like to trumpet how they make such topics 'relevant,' 'engaging,' 'fun.' But if there is relevance, engagement or fun, it is in spite of such topics and the torpor they rightly induce.

What can The Great Fire of London really mean to a five-year-old? Nothing. What can it matter? Not at all. Is the stench of scorched wood hanging in the classroom air? Are the wails of its dying poor to be heard through the classroom walls? Is its heat searing through the classroom windows? Are its ashes drying out the children's tongues? Is there even any smoke to be seen? If there is no smoke, there is no fire. There is no smoke and there is no Great Fire of London; nothing to be smelt, heard, touched, tasted or seen, only something to be looked at, only something to be known.

What are the children learning, then, as they get to know, aged five, about The Great Fire of London? Certainly, they are gaining nothing that might count for an understanding of The Great Fire of London, for all that some may end by saying the name 'Pepys' and others, perhaps, by spelling the word 'London.' Neither, however, are they learning nothing at all. In fact, they are being given a quite fundamental lesson, which they are – such a pity! – following closely and well: a lesson in disregarding what is real and all about them, salient and lived; a lesson in the importance of what is not real and all about them, not salient and lived, of abstract events and concepts not near to them at all.

The children are learning what they will continue to learn forever: to be prised away from what they can easily, naturally, touch, smell, taste, hear and see, so that they may attend to that which cannot be touched, smelt, tasted, heard or seen. They are learning, in short, to take those steps back – baby steps to begin with, of course – so that all they will ever seek out is a better, which is to say a more remote, look at things than their mere senses can provide.

Joseph, aged five, was already 'out' as autistic, already exempt from The Great Fire of London. No one corrected him when he wandered off to flick through a book from the shelves, nor did they call his attention when his eyes glazed over. But how many more of the children had joined him, by the time The Great Fire of

London had burnt itself out that half-term? How many more had had their attention span eroded beyond recall? In how many more pairs of eyes had the light dimmed?

Not all, of course. There were survivors, even of The Great Fire of London, hardy types, who managed to sustain a lively interest in the world around them. But if there were these resilient ones, who came through the ordeal unscathed, they did so immediately to endure another like it, as they transitioned from The Great Fire of London to whatever was the next topic to be looked at: Great Explorers, perhaps, or Life on the Ocean Wave.

The particular theme hardly matters, so long as it features like something between a bauble and a bullet on that document known as The Curriculum: a rigid and meaningless collection of materials; an engineered substitute for whatever might present itself to be learnt in an actual, not a simulated, real life; that great step back from anything that might be engaged with as part of a vernacular culture; that amputation of involvement that it is the purpose of our institutions of education to effect, which makes all learning into distance learning and renders all content remote.

And the institutions leave nothing to chance. There might still have been survivors, after all, a small handful valiantly undefeated by Great Explorers and by Life on the Ocean Wave, and by the hundred other topics rolled out to be known. A few still interested in life. A few still with light in their eyes. There might have been, if the buck stopped at The Curriculum. But it does not. Up on the whiteboard of Joseph's classroom – about half-way through The Great Fire of London – was written the word for the day: 'success.' My heart chilled. For, I knew what was coming. In the classroom next door, where the six-year-olds are taught, up on the whiteboard every day is written: 'We will be successful today if…' By the time they reach seven – the age of reason we used to be told – the children are prefacing every task they undertake by identifying its 'success criteria,' stepping back from The Curriculum to look at what counts as involvement with it. Stepping back from the stepping back, Looking at the looking. Getting distance from the distance. Even the hardiest specimens cannot withstand it.

If they could, it would not matter anyway. For, the school is now all but without its walls, The Curriculum seeping out to infect the whole of our children's day, which they never cease to have to step back from and look at, which they live, or pretend to live, remotely. This is not only because so much of our children's out-of-school time is spent in school-like institutions, in nurseries and breakfast clubs and after-school clubs, and in organised recreation of all kinds. And it is not only because the toys that they play with are overdetermined by educational content – The Curriculum, painted up to look like a jigsaw or programmed to seem like a game. And it is not only because they play with those toys – in the company of, or encouraged by, adults – almost all of their non-scheduled day, in which they have scarcely a moment of informal time to look about them. It is also because even the few apparently informal events and interactions that remain to our children have been made rigid and meaningless by their aping the abstractions of school.

How many times have I overheard a parent *explaining* things to his child, stepping back from whatever the situation is and trying to take his young child with him. *What do we do when Daddy asks us how our day has been? What do we say when Granny gives us a gift? Remember, just because we can do something does not mean that we should do it.* Nothing imparted implicitly as a specific and lived experience; everything explicated as an impersonal lesson, complete with its success criterion. The airwaves, filled with reasoning, with poorly articulated ethical principles of the most general kind. It makes for wearying listening, as Daddy strains to deliver what are complex philosophical lessons. *Why do we always treat other people kindly?* – Immanuel Kant could not solve this abstract problem, even at the height of his powers. Yet we burden our young children with the conundrum. Little wonder they grow so fractious and demanding. Little wonder they drift off aimlessly still sobbing their by-rote tears. Continuously bombarded by far-too-abstract rules of a far-too-complex game, forever plucked from out of the reality in which they might be involved to confront stakes in which they have not even a remote interest, little wonder they flip flop between hyperactivity and disaffection, between the hysteria and the jadedness that are the earliest signs of the onset of ASD.

*

Meanwhile, Joseph was still at the bookshelves, flicking intently through one of his favourites, on the eighth page of which was a familiar and absorbing tear. Or his eyes were still glazed over, as he listened – more carefully than the rest of us know how – to the 'o' sound in his teacher's regional speech, which he would produce later to good effect. How we wished that he would attend to what was happening. How we hoped that he would gradually get involved. And yet, was there anything happening? Was there any possibility of involvement? The Great Fire of London was certainly not happening. The Great Fire of London was an assault upon involvement – a remote event presented remotely. Joseph's wandering off was highly appropriate, after all – *there's nothing to see here folks, or to hear or touch or smell or taste or feel.* It was the other children who were vulnerable during The Great Fire of London, bereft as they were of any protection against the systematic assault upon their sense of reality that comprises what we call their education.

You cannot *explain* anything to a young child with autism, who is gloriously immune to explanation. You cannot look at anything with a young child with autism, who is gloriously unable to look. If there is someone to model it with her, she can do some painting, say – she might be very good at doing some painting. What she cannot do is step back from painting, look at painting, look at herself painting, look behind the back of painting. She cannot paint remotely. If you ask her to, she will already have lost interest. If others are doing it around her, she will already have wandered off.

And why would she not? Have you looked behind the back of painting? Have you seen how dull it is? Have you compared its beige monotony with the shapes and shades on its other side? Never mind painting – what of fire? Is there anything more absorbing, to child and adult alike, than lighting a fire? A whole life may be lived in the achievement, and the glory of its success has not a moment of same. Even a match to light a candle will do it – and blowing it out is a birthday every time. But The Great Fire of London, that remote fire taught remotely? No better than the back side of the canvas: without heat, without light, with neither char nor crackle; dull, so dull, uninvolving, uninteresting; a travesty of real fire, good only for replacing those hearts that might have been warmed with heads as cold as facts. The result: boredom, for the most part; and a weary capacity to disbelieve that there might be something at which to toast our hands and feet.

I once ate Christmas dinner next to a log fire that was burning on a wall-mounted flat-screen TV. A 'fire' that was 'burning': the quotation marks are all, bracketing off the fire and its burning, distilling the essence of the fire and its burning, by which is always intended that which the fire and its burning *look like*. Trading on our cultivated disbelief that experiences delivered through our senses are of much significance, premised on our knowledge society in which only cold abstractions are highly rated, the flat-screen fire is allowed to burn, and to console those from whom the real world retreats with its cold two-dimensional comfort. It might as well have been The Great Fire of London. I looked at it only once before I was as dead to it as it was to me. And as soon as I could, I wandered off to the bookshelves, to console myself by flicking through familiar pages.

From what was I seeking escape? From that delight, shared among my Christmas crowd, in the paltry flat-screen abstraction, in its being enough of fire for us all to be getting on with, in its contempt for the smell and the soot of what might have been. This dull beige look behind the back of fire, this remote fire, abroad somehow as more than a real fire could be. We are coached, not only to step back from sensory experiences, not only to look at what lies behind them, but to crow over this stepping back and this looking. The boredom of dull abstraction is accompanied by the triumph of dull abstraction, as we fondle the hand that starves us. *We are not taken in. We are not impressed. We are au fait*, so fully aware of the nuts and bolts of things, of what they are really about – so cynical.

Our knowledge society is really our knowing society, our *we all know* society; we, who are too good to believe in what lies before us; we, who are forever looking behind the back of things; we, who are never fooled; we, who know it all. No coincidence that Ladybird's 'How It Works' series has been one of the publishing phenomena of our century, which apes Ladybird's 1950s ingenuous descriptions of, say, the engine of a car, with entirely disingenuous descriptions of The Car, and The Husband, and The Date, and The Meeting, and so on. Perhaps The Painting will be next. Or The Fire.

We smile at these books, as we do at an in-joke, which is always at someone's expense. And maybe we cry at the flat-screen blaze. But these moments of delight and despair are only the margins of what is our standard fare. Laugh or cry, this is what we have learnt to be good at: this never taking things at face value, this never sitting in the immediacy of lived experience, this rendering things into abstractions that we never tire of and are so very tired of at the same time.

And the child with autism just cannot learn how to do it. He cannot step back, not even far enough to see that Patrick is his brother. Ladybird's *The Brother* is not a book over which he can laugh or cry. He cannot laugh, because he is not cynical and will not be placed in that holding pattern of disbelief into which we initiate even very young children, to languish there the whole of their lives. And he cannot cry, because he has been crying almost all of his young life, at the rigidity and the meaninglessness of our hollow concepts of reality, which he is constantly encouraged to attend to and get involved in, even though they are so very remote. But he knows better. He knows that Patrick is Patrick: unsullied, unfiltered, as pure and as particular – as real – as he can be.

*

Or he *would* know this, would keep knowing this, if there was not another prong to our society's assault upon our experience of reality, another aspect to its endless spiral of abstraction, from which even the child with autism is not exempt.

Reality itself, and not only our experience of reality, is not immune to being remade. The abstractions that accumulate before it change not only our capacity to access it; they change it. Its vibrancy slowly haemorrages through the portal that we open up in its fourth wall, as we step back from it, ever further, to take a better look.

Our cynicism is gradually written into the reality that we are cynical about, a reality that itself grows so cynical as to consign everyone, including the child with autism, to trying to squeeze an experience from out of a dry, mostly theoretical, scene. From learning to disbelieve what is right before our eyes, what is right before our eyes become unbelievable, unavailable to our senses for the most part, or available only as a flat-screen version of what it might have been, combining that heady perfect-match with our key concepts that causes in us a hysteria of belonging with an anaemic thinness that is so deeply unsatisfying and dull. The result is hyperstimulation and disaffection, the earliest signs of ASD.

Ground zero of *real* The Great Fire of London was Thomas Farriner's baker's shop. It was the kind of establishment that might have been found on every street in seventeenth-century London, the aroma of its daily bread doing battle with the smell of the river and of the sewage that flowed past its door, selling its produce for everyman's enjoyment of skillfully rendered crust and crumb. At the heart of The Great Fire of London: a baker's shop, whose flames made kindling of the medieval timbers of Pudding Lane. A point of 'relevance' for the children, no? After all, even a five-year-old eats bread. Even a five-year-old knows the meaning of bread.

Or does he? Is even this staple, which might have been an on-ramp for the five-year-olds to The Great Fire of London, cordoned off by the prevailing unreality that circulates in our society? The most popular brand of bread in the UK is produced by the company Warburten's, whose food products are outsold in the UK only by that bastion of the abstract, Coca Cola, and whose bread is that familiar sliced-up-in-plastic variety that is stacked in heaps on the shelves of our supermarkets and local shops, bread produced in factories far removed from our houses and our streets and that emits no smell for us as it bakes, bread that lands on our plate as if from outer space. Yes, it looks like bread. But it does not feel like anything but the idea of bread, proven quickly with more yeast than is good for us, made with flour made from wheat bred for its sturdiness and patent, sodden with the sugar and the salt that have killed our sense of taste with their kindness. We reach for a slice of this bread and our hand sinks into its implausible cushion, its glutenous pap. This is abstract bread, a form where bread should be but is not, duping our body's senses in a charade of real experience that fatally dulls their edge.

When we buy this bread, we are cynics. When we toast this bread, we are cynics. When we eat this bread, we are cynics. For, this is cynical bread, one of the infinite number of products of a cynical system that is so destructive of real experiences that only our imputations of them remain. And all of that 'proper' bread, baked by artisans and sold to the cobbled together connoisseurship of our shrinking middle-classes? That too is abstract bread, bread that steps back from bread to get a better look at bread, even more fulsomely than a Warburten's or its like. Bread into which not a single gram of uncynical yeast has been added, nor a single unknowing knead has been applied. Like the 'organic' food and the 'health' food which it signals loudly as its virtue, it has won its unique selling point from the defeat of the life of food. There is abstract bread that will do you no good and abstract bread that will do you some good; but there is now only abstract bread – bread with the life sucked out of it.

And this is just bread. Roll out this remaking of reality according to abstractions in any direction you like, and you will gain an understanding of the rigidity and the meaninglessness of what passes for life in our society, as even the most intimate of relations is clogged by key ideas, easily circulated concepts which engineer a so-called 'reality' that is ever more freely available for reengineering in the latest generic and convenient image. We 'hashtag' these key concepts and distribute them as attachments to carefully constructed facsimiles of life. *#love*. *#instagood*. *#happy*. *#girl*: some of the more frequently applied key concepts of our time. *#bread* is not on the list, but *#food* is there in all its undifferentiating glory.

There are many, many such key concepts, some more pernicious than others. I write easily here of the 'child' with autism. Yet, 'child' is one of the most stultifying key concepts of our times. This may rankle – children are real, surely, and not just engineered. Well, yes, children are real. But realities, we may recall, *arise*; and in our society they mostly arise as engineered instances of abstract concepts.

Consider who it is these 'children' are, to whom we refer so naturally – key concepts thrive in the consoling air of what comes naturally. We know them now for their being dressed up like children, in such an array of colours and patterns that any gathering of children looks like a mock-up of some corporate advertisement. In times and places other than ours, young people wear and have worn a version of what older people wear and have worn; but we dress our young people up as children, and every day is a dress-up day, and the costumes come with accessories of all kinds: coloured and printed helmets and backpacks and lunch bags and cases for technology and water bottles and wellington boots and wetsuits. Having donned their costumes, our young people are brought forth to play their part, to act like children, in spaces designed to produce childlike behaviour – soft-play centres and sand pits and themed parks of every kind, which spaces only make sense if you act like a child, if you gambol aimlessly and shout without purpose. And the soft surfaces and the sand remake our young people's gait, eroding the equilibrium that has only just been won with a return to unsteadiness and ungainliness, limbs sinking into quicksand so that a second childhood runs concurrently with the first. Our young people walk like children, and they talk like children too: in the voices of the computer-generated chipmunk-creatures that feature on the screens that we place before them more persistently than it is possible to believe.

We enroll our young people in an extended advertisement of childhood, a promotion of childhood to them and us all, which employs carefully researched strategies for subliminal messaging, for nudging us to experience children as if they are real: colours suggesting innocence; tones of voice implying vulnerability; movements invoking the impulse to protect…all aimed at the remaking or our young people in the image of a hi-definition #*child*.

When older people use those chipmunk voices back to their young people, and push and carry them when they could walk, and screen them when they could observe, and put them into spaces that crystallize the inanity of their condition, what we deny to them is: an un-childlike scene into which they might look and from which they might learn; the seriousness that might attach to those with the largest amount of future at their feet; the newness and originality and, yes, the innocence that they might have brought to bear on our old world. For, our young people, though children, are not innocent. Our young people, because they are children, are hopelessly cynical, living breathing step-backs from youth so that it might the better look like a perfect childhood.

And it is school that is most responsible in all of this: where we sequester young people who are therefore excused from the cut and thrust of life, to spend their days, among others like themselves, forming the habits of a childhood that is deemed to be their natural condition, and being emptied of that energetic curiosity and involvement that is their rightful condition, stumbling about in small loud voices rather than observing and organizing as they might do so well. If left for a moment to themselves, even still their seriousness may begin to surface – how gravely they set up their game of cricket, or arrange their den, or make a spaceship out of cardboard, or dress the bed as they've seen you do it. But we do not leave them a moment to themselves; even their 'breaks' are dimmed by surveillance and confined to times and spaces so tight as to allow no lightness in at all.

Our schools, it turns out, are at the epicentre of a two-pronged move to abstraction. On the one hand, schools prepare the ground for the implantation of all manner of engineered concepts by readying young people, who would become involved with a stick if you let them, for their removal from sensory existence, by always having their eyes turned to theoretical matters as rendered on the pages of textbooks or websites; they may subsequently get 'practical,' of course – build The Great Fire of London out of crepe paper, perhaps – but the horse, by then, has bolted, the senses being well under control. On the other hand, schools work to produce one specific abstract reality. Schools produce the 'child': to generate which we shackle those among us who are least satisfied with abstraction and consign them to an out-of-life institution, to a half-life of non-conversing, non-deciding, non-serious, non-learning not-yetness; and by which we notionally empty into a segment of human existence all of the energy and innocence and audacity that is denied to us in our adult lives and whose denial we accept because we remember that we experienced energy and innocence and audacity in our childhood but that we have now put away our childish things. But we did not experience energy and innocence and audacity in our childhood, only submitted to the engineered version of them produced in and circulated by our schools.

School weaves the curtain of childhood and draws it over our young people. Behind this curtain, they are engineered as one of our major abstract realities and simultaneously prepared to submit to abstract realities during the whole of the rest of their lives.

And young people with autism will not learn what school tries to teach them. They will not be engineered as the abstract reality that we call a 'child' and they will not be prepared to submit to abstract realities. A double refusal, to counter school's double assault. A living, breathing rejection: of the rigid persona in which the vital energies of youth are entombed; of the low-meaning realities with which the gamut of sensory experiences are replaced. Young people with autism are a living indictment of school.

*

Where, then, are our young people to learn? What is to become of their reading, writing and arithmetic, and their geography and history and science? To what manner of life would we sentence them by denying them their right to be schooled?

A first response to these questions might be a statement of the persistent and increasing failure of our schools to facilitate young people in learning what it is they go to school to learn. Data produced in 2019 by the National Literacy Trust in the UK shows that sixteen percent of adults in the UK – nine million in all – are functionally illiterate, unable to understand the instructions on their prescribed medicine, for example. This, despite all such adults having matured in a society in which universal primary and secondary education was not only available but compulsory. In the US, the situation is even worse – the government's department for education there reports that between twenty and twenty-three percent of adults are functionally illiterate, with just under twenty percent of high-school graduates unable to read what is written on their certificate of graduation. And this is only functional illiteracy, a fairly low threshold of competence with the spoken and written word. How many of those who finish their schooling could even begin to interpret Plato's parable of the cave is miniscule and shrinking. And the data tells us that numeracy is even less well-served by our schools.

Schools, then, are not very good at teaching us to read and write and add-up, never mind at encouraging our involvement – 'engagement' is the key word here – in what we read and write and add-up. Really, they do not even pretend to be good at it, constantly declaring, through the media and government institutions, their persistent failures in this regard. What they do claim to be good at is the invention and documentation of procedures for the improvement of literacy and numeracy and engagement. In fact, reform of itself at every level, in order to address its failures, is just what school is for.

When you have a young person with 'special needs,' the failure that defines our schools is quite apparent: you attend meeting after meeting, sometimes with staff members who are genuinely committed to promoting your child's learning, at which are discussed new, often poorly thought out though theoretically interesting, methods for the promotion of your child's education; these methods will, in the weeks and months ahead, generate swathes of observation and documentation, but their implementation, if it happens much at all, will be patchy, unsustained and oriented almost wholly to the production of documentary evidence of its implementation, for submission to funding pots or to regulatory bodies of various kinds. In the midst of all of this, your child with 'special needs' is little more than an occasion for the invention and documentation of 'best-practices,' and often a rather too imperfect occasion, contributing less than document-ready instances of 'best-practices' at work.

Like other institutions of their kind, schools continually step back from themselves to take a better look at what they do, so that teaching young people to read is less important than stepping back from and looking at the teaching of young people to read. The more steps back, the worse the reading. It makes sense when you set it out. But the important thing has been that we do not make sense of it, that we continue in the blind panic and urge for reform that always leads to another step back and to more looking, and that positions the young person learning to read at a greater and greater distance from the possibility.

Ask yourself this: where was it that you learned almost everything that you have learnt? Was it really in school? I spent many years in compulsory and post-compulsory education and yet the number of things that I learned from it is negligible. Years spent with my head bowed over problems in mathematical differentiation – What *is* mathematical differentiation? Years spent learning passages from history books about Ancient Rome and the Spanish Civil War – can I tell you anything now about either? Did I, even at the time, have any sense of the significance of Ancient Rome or the Spanish Civil War? The life-cycle of the worm. Farming practices in the Mezzogiorno. English translations of Old Irish folklore. Ox-bo lakes. So many hours – so many of the most potentially vital years of my life – with my back bent over pages of writing that I learned well enough to reproduce in correct examination format and never had any idea of involvement with at all.

What I have learnt has almost all been learnt outside of school, in daily life, in conversation with others, in trial and error: the hollow sound of a loaf of bread that is cooked; the right time to stop adding stock to a risotto; how to parallel-park a car; how to plumb beneath a kitchen sink; what it means to reject the dualism that confounds our Western culture; how best to communicate the insights of Sartre to a class of eighteen-year-olds; the offside rule in football; how to succeed in making a young person with autism sit at the table for dinner; how to operate an Excel spreadsheet...None of this learnt at school; none of this requiring the days and weeks and years spent slumped in school, days and weeks and years during which I might have learnt so very much more than I have managed to do since.

But this possibility, of learning outside of school, is more or less closed to young people now. Now, the walls of the school have come away. Now, there is only school-learning, which is to say learning in which you cannot become involved in any way, which is to say no real learning at all. You cannot learn what a hollow sound is until you have undercooked twenty loaves of bread – and very little bread is baked in the school without walls. The right time to add stock to a risotto can be learnt only after a dozen chalky risottos have been served and reluctantly eaten – and very little risotto is cooked in the school without walls. Perhaps we still learn to park a car, although prompts from the vehicle itself are preparing us for the self-driving future in which we will not learn this either. We might learn how to plumb beneath the kitchen sink, except that the ease with which we now throw out one kitchen and replace it with another leaves the plumbing only slight opportunity to malfunction. There is no chance whatsoever of realizing the dualism of Western culture, since to do so requires an experience of embodiment more intense than anything available in the abstract environment of the school without walls (dualism militates against its own discovery). One no longer assists eighteen-year-olds to understand the insights of Sartre, but only to know them in their key-concept translation onto a PowerPoint screen. Not even referees are now trusted to apply the offside rule, because the technology will mostly tell them different. And the prompts to support your young person with autism will never be repeated as often as they need to be (twice or three times a day over three years, perhaps) to end in his sitting at the table for dinner, because parents do not have the time and institutions do not have the will and children, being 'children,' must eat as and when they wish to anyway.

You will, however, learn to fill in an Excel spreadsheet – in the school without walls, that is what remains...the much-heralded 'tech skills,' which render us as masters of portals to the world wide web, phones and tablets so user-friendly as to respond to our merest touch. Children at school get good practice at this touch, as they negotiate the latest 'apps' on their 'Ipads.' But this touch is decidedly not the *grasp* that is our body-metaphor – alas now only a metaphor – for real learning. When you at last attune your ear to the hollow sound of a cooked loaf, you have grasped what hollow really means – it is in your body, it is in your ear, unlike anything that you only know remotely. You shall not forget it, as you shall not forget how to ride a bike. Truly, you have it. To grasp something is a fulsome achievement. Risky too, of course, without the safety guaranteed by abstraction:

whatever it is you try to grasp may kick back at you, sting you, burn you, cut you, tear you; those twenty under-cooked loaves are not easy to digest. The touch that we use on the screens of our 'tech' is without any risk at all, being just about as active an erasure of our body as can be achieved by a bodily gesture. My mother cannot sink even to that contempt for her body necessary to use an old-style computer 'mouse,' although she can do the finest needlework. And anyone who does not own a 'smart' phone will tell you how diluted our grasp must be to operate them. How degrading, this dilution! How contemptuous of our bodies! And our young people are learning it before they learn anything else, despite well-established research on the degradation of their dexterity by their early initiation into the barely-touch. The risk returns, after all: not the honest risk of a cut or a sting on the hand that is brought to bear on the world; but the insidious risk of atrophy of muscles that are no longer brought to bear on the world at all.

(How sad, that the surfaces into which our children's limbs sink as into quicksand, which have made their legs so knock-kneed and ungainly, are complimented by surfaces along which their fingertips skate so slightly as to cause them to wither from lack of use.)

Our school without walls amounts to nothing less than the engineering of our world out of any possibility of real involvement with it, of real engagement, real learning. Substituted for this possibility, which has constituted human cultures throughout history, is the infinitely thinner necessity of that round of transmission of abstract concepts that is all that remains to us of a culture, but which is only the back-side of a culture, a step back from anything that might crystallize as a culture. In fact, our school-without-walls society relinquishes the horizons of a real culture in its dazzlement at the prospect of a step-back so fulsome as to offer us a global perspective, dispensing with those frameworks within which lived projects might involve us in favour of a world of abstract possibilities which have no particular interest in us and in which it is beyond us to gain any real purchase. There can be no grasping anything in such a society; it will hardly endure our lightest touch. We tip-toe across it as if we are light as a feather, as if our bodies weigh nothing at all. We are impatient for this tip-toe to bring forth for us the wide world, but the wide world captures without consoling, ensnares without engaging, and chills us by its cold remoteness.

And we know it. Or we feel it, at any rate. In our craving for something more. In our starving for something real. The health institutions are there, of course, when this craving gets too much. Ready to give the health-treatment to the effects of an education that has prepared us to accept such treatment – what a vicious circle that one is! Ready with one of its labels, to discover something deep down inside us and prevent our seeking the source of our ills in our world. 'Derealization' or

'Depersonalization': you can take your pick. And you will. And you will be eased, for a time, by having arrived at a truth. But still the craving returns. Still, we are starved by abstraction. In 2019, the most common word in the short biographies posted by users of the dating platform Tinder was the word 'real,' as they sought, in their millions, to squeeze something meaningful from out of the cardboard cut-outs they skim past in their jaded hysteria, and lent their virtual voices to clamour in unison for the one thing that is needed to light the fire of love: the supple richness of bodied interaction, up close and personal, not distant, not remote.

*

Sometimes, I have looked in at Joseph as he and his classmates have played in the schoolyard. Joseph has always been alone. Climbing on the equipment, alone. Skipping around the edge of the yard, alone. Singing, alone. Could anything be more affecting? To see my little boy – so sweet as I know him to be – without a friend, without the prospect of a friend, while his fellows gambol past in twos and threes, indifferent to him and to his world. But I no longer feel very sad at this scene. For one thing, I know that Joseph at present does not feel sad in it. I know that he has no longing for the company of his classmates. That he has no idea that he might share in their games. But mostly, I am not sad because the hum in which his play takes no part is not the melody of youthful energy and innocence, and the voices among which his does not sound are neither frank nor divinely enigmatic – there is no heartfelt laughter, no musical vibration, no demure murmur, only cartoon raucousness and fractious disappointment and, yes, a yearning bewilderment. What is poignant is not that Joseph stands apart from this hyperbolic, this garishly patterned, this desperately distanced, crowd, but that so very many number in it.

4

Care

Some time ago, I received a phone call from the teaching assistant who supports Joseph during his school day. The phone call was about the application of lip balm to Joseph's lips. A banality, to be sure. And yet, those who care for a child with autism will know that no detail in the cut and thrust of daily life is too banal to become of material importance to the comfort of everyone around.

That morning, I had noticed that Joseph was beginning to suffer from chapped lips – in the windy northeast of England, not very unusual. Everybody knows, of course, that if you do not apply a protective balm you have to be very disciplined indeed to resist the urge to moisten chapped lips with your tongue; everybody also knows that this serves only to worsen their condition. As with many aspects of life, however, this mundane one, when in play in the context of autism, is potentially much more serious.

It is not possible to explain to Joseph that he must not lick his lips. If you are in time, you can apply the appropriate balm, although it is also not possible to explain to Joseph that he ought not to rub this off immediately. Neither is this something that you can simply, physically, prevent him from doing, as you can prevent his dismounting a chair, for instance. You can hold back his arms to stop him, but he cannot, during that time of restraint, be brought to accept it as he can be brought to accept having to remain on a chair; the call of the sensory is too overwhelming, and the distress of being asked to ignore that call is too profound.

The hope, then, is that you have caught the drying lips in time, that your applications of balm are sufficiently frequent, and that the residue that remains from its being every time wiped away is enough to soothe and defuse the situation. If things do not work out well, the chapped lips become sore within a few hours, at which point Joseph adds to his constant licking of them an equally constant rubbing at them with his sleeve, which causes them to become more sore, and leads him to begin to be distressed by this soreness and to indicate that he would like it to go away, although any attempt to soothe it – applying some kind of cream – will be resisted and cause further distress and will be undone by more immediate rubbing. The worst result is that a large patch of Joseph's face, around his mouth, becomes cracked and bleeding, affecting his ability to eat and drink comfortably and generally to be in the world with any ease, none of which can be discussed with him or explained to him. The whole affair can last for as long as two weeks.

With all of that in mind, on the morning in question I applied a balm to Joseph's lips a few times before school. When we arrived at the doorway of his classroom and were met by his teaching assistant, I explained the situation, applied more balm myself then and there, and handed over the tub, indicating that it should be used regularly throughout the day. Joseph's assistant was aware of the potential gravity of the situation, and readily agreed.

Then, later that morning, I received the phone call, letting me know that, having seen the tub of lip balm being produced and used, another teacher had questioned whether lip balm was named in Joseph's file as a product that could be applied to his skin and whether I had signed any document that proved that I was accepting of such a product being applied by designated members of staff at the school. The answer to these questions was no, and so the call was made to inform me that no further application of balm could be made to Joseph's lips without my having first signed a paper to testify that this was something that I agreed to. I drove to the school, was talked through a printed form, which I signed, after which the balm was used as I wished it to be, but over an hour had passed in the interim, during which Joseph's lips had deteriorated from lack of attention, and a situation that might have lasted for one day went on to last for about five days.

Hardly less disturbing during those five days than the sight of Joseph's broken lips was the consciousness of what had made them so, the defining aspects of this so-banal slice of his institutional care.

Most defining: the abdication of care, for the sake of a more explicit enterprise, an enterprise that, unlike the lowly duties of care, admits of protocols and their documentation, regulation, assessment and review. This enterprise is an offshoot of care, or it would seem to be, but is really so anathema as to suck the life out of care by remaking it as fit for insertion into institutional boxes. This is the enterprise, not of care but of *safety*, an achievement that is apparently related to care – perhaps even to the most careful of care – but that goes against the grain of care in its mission to define that which must be indistinct and to pin down that which only runs free.

*

The enterprise of safety is a busy one – of that there can be no doubt. Indeed, busyness is its most salient characteristic. We are not to accuse our officers of safety of that brand of neglect of care that arises from inertia – Joseph's lips were left to dry out in the classroom's stale air, not from apathy or inattention but from energetic meticulousness. There is much ado about keeping one another safe. It is a kind of bustle.

Why this bustle? Because keeping one another safe involves the assiduous identification and mitigation of something that is all around us all the time, something that demands the careful planning of the strategist and the unrelenting alertness of the sniper, something increasingly touted as avoidable and to be avoided and fear of not avoiding which lends to every instance of its planned avoidance and recorded avoidance the heady sensation of salvation, of having come through this time, of having lived to tell the tale. Staying safe is the ongoing battle with *risk*, a multi-fronted fight of such satisfying detail to the planners amongst us and such intoxicating bombast to the doers amongst us that the banality of plain old care, to be neither planned for nor heralded, traded implicitly between ourselves, has little to recommend it.

Care is essentially personal – up close and personal, to be precise. It is one-on-one, proximate. Joseph's lips needed to be touched, needed the balm to be smeared on them, right into their corners. Such banal and intimate ministrations. Yet, the banality and the intimacy are care's essential features, its duties fulfilled at the point of contact and always needing to be seen to again – apply the balm, and apply it again when it has soaked in, and apply it again when it has been licked away, and apply it again when it has been rubbed away, and apply it again after lunchtime, and apply it again before going home... The interactions of care are lowly for sure, but they require to unfold without impediment, their easy repetition constituting the difference between one day and five days of six-year-old misery.

Do not conclude that its lowly repetitions imply that care is predictable. On the contrary, care refuses the rigidity of the plan, the programme, the protocol, and the pathway. Because it is personal, because its interactions are so vitally meaningful, care is also an ad hoc achievement, regulated by the judgment that comes of experience and that knows when to stop or to go again or to do something different this time. Unlike the rigid routines of safety, with all their bustle and their bombast, practices of care circulate modestly and wisely, a quiet call and response that is far too indistinct to be captured and regulated on the institutions' unyielding forms.

Care, then, is the opposite of ASD: where our autistic society would block meaningful interactions by mediating them through risk assessments and safety procedures, care reaches out to touch the skin, to feel the brow, to rub the head, to hold the hand, establishing points of contact for the circulation of our solicitude for one another; and where our autistic society would devise a scheme for every eventuality so that our lives with one another are not so much lived as carried out, care adjusts itself to life as it unfolds, in all its contingency, its subtlety, its specificity.

But there is worse.

The great bustle of stamping out risk is surely a sad suspension of the meaningful interaction and the circumstantial judgment that are needed for care – while Joseph's teachers were checking the medical forms in the school's filing cabinet and debating the safety or otherwise of proceeding to apply balm to his lips and deciding to make the phone call and retrieving my number from the database and printing out the relevant form and waiting to meet me and talk me through the protocol, Joseph sat in the classroom, rubbing his cracked lips into days of discomfort and upset.

But the mission of staying safe does not only suspend the circulation of care; staying safe actively militates against care. Once safety is established as our institutions' bottom line, care itself comes to be deemed unsafe. For, care's essentially unpredictable character and care's demand for personal proximity are the very 'problems' that risk management is bent on solving - every contingency must be 'covered,' that is, made predictable and subject to impersonal response.

The pursuit of safety, in other words, is aimed directly against the possibility of care, insofar as the pursuit of safety would roll out ASD as a condition of us all: looking to turn whatever occurs meaningfully between us as we live our lives into something that unfolds impersonally between anyone fulfilling their 'role'; and looking to turn whatever requires well-judged immediate responses into something that plays out predictably and according to preset routines.

Are we such a long way from ASD's obsession with safety going so far as to reframe care as, simply, unsafe? Are we very far from ASD's taking pride in the abdication of care? Are we not in fact close to the ultimate triumph of ASD, when the designation of care as a risky business becomes the advertisement of lack of care as proof of safety? Once ASD culminates to that degree, our retreat from the contact necessary for care will be undertaken with a great eclat, as the best proof available of our collective devotion to safety.

Our officers of safety even now begin to prevail on these grounds: their contempt for the modest attentions of care, circulated too quietly and closely between ourselves to allow for documentation and review, and their sense of the greater sophistication of procedures conducted formally and without contact, procedures dictated by the demands of dead documents and not by the needs of living bodies, tending to drown out in their showy certainties the low hum turning-over of care.

*

What can explain this alarming triumph of ASD over care? When it implies the sacrifice of the warmest of interactions – those in which we touch one another? When it involves reneging upon the most well-adjusted of ministrations – those in which we judge the situation and act accordingly? Why is it that the pursuit of safety wins the day? When staying safe means standing back and sticking to the plan, how can it trump the benefits and the joys of coming close and seeing how it goes?

To solve this conundrum, it is necessary only to ask: what is it that you can only do by staying safe, by reneging upon the modest and unpredictable duties of care in order to pursue a perceived advantage that is impersonal and predictable? What do you get when you step out of the risky reach of human touch, and administer others from a distance and according to the rules?

The answer lies in the high visibility that comes with impersonal distance and rigid regulations – the possibility for display of our concern for others and our aptitude in assuaging this concern. The close proximity and ad hoc nature of care do not admit of this possibility; you cannot show off to those whose bodies you can touch, and you cannot make a display of decisions that are made and acted upon in the moment.

The great recompense of trading care for safety is that it allows us to *signal* our righteousness, to show it, to measure out how much we *really care* and then declare it to the world.

Care, by its nature, is mostly hidden. It is, for this reason, a thorn in the side of our increasingly autistic sensibilities, which require rigid markers not implicit understanding and whose impulse is always to refract our interactions through some apparently neutral sign system, though such a system works mostly to block those interactions under the aegis of their mere refraction.

It is this that explains the debacle of Joseph's lip balm, as the banal add-on duty of applying it a few times to his chapped lips was so readily forsaken for the opportunity to signal how good his school is at keeping its students safe, in the ready-and-waiting slots on generic documents, appropriate for submission to regulatory bodies that have the remit to award a school as 'outstanding' if the signals of its really caring are sufficiently loud and clear. Nothing hidden, nothing unacknowledged, nothing unrewarded: the unhistorical practices of care exchanged for the blazoning signals of our staying safe.

Care is being suffocated, literally right before our eyes, by our growing need to be seen to care. No care is care enough now that it is not its hyperbolic signal; no care is care enough now that is not to be seen and from afar; no care is care enough now that is not the highly visible promise of our safety.

High-visibility is a well-established trope in our society, our gaze long blinded by swathes of neon – armbands and gilets and jackets and backpacks and bottles and hats and gloves and socks and shoes, worn at all times of the day and night, under the highest of suns and in the most remote of country retreats. As if visibility, unaugmented, is not visible enough. As if one is hidden in plain sight, unseen and therefore unsafe. The potent link between being seen and being safe is forged. Our common-or-garden being in the world, not seen enough so not safe enough – not on the commons, not in the gardens. Groups of children in the morning light, skipping in high-visibility hand-in-hand the few short steps from their breakfast club to their school.

Only the chance that keeping safe affords us to show how much we *really care* can explain this garish excess;

only our growing need to show that we care, to see that we care, to wear our caring hearts on our sleeves.

To be seen, you must be at a distance. To broadcast more widely, you must be at a greater distance. *Stand back so that you can see me. Now look! – see how much I care!*

But care is up close. Care is personal. Care does not happen from a distance. Care unfolds within arm's reach.

In the UK at least, the mantra of midwives and mothers-to-be is 'skin-to-skin' with your baby and not a moment to lose. Talk is of forming a bond, of easing anxieties and of protecting against infection. But does the great urgency with which it is spoken of betray an underlying awareness that care must be established quickly now, before all hope of connection is lost, before this new being loses its immunity to signal, for which immunity we pine without knowing it. We crave our own renewal by this virgin life, gloriously unable to see: to forgo, for a few precious moments, the heavy work of being seen to care and, simply, to care.

We know it, that care lives on the skin, that to care needs the touch of skin to skin – even if our rush to establish that care in the moments immediately after birth shows that we also sense, and desperately, that the chance to care does not now come often and does not now last long.

*

What of young people with autism in all of this? What of those who do not much like to look, even to see how much we really care? What of those who need to touch? Do they notice our signals? Do they know that we are keeping them safe?

Or do they even care?

Someone I know, who works as a coordinator of autism support in a secondary school, quickly summarized what autistic people are like: *On a Monday morning, all my students come in and say 'Hi Miss, how was your weekend?' It's just that the autistic ones couldn't care less about my weekend.*

From someone in her job, it was a dispiriting summary of autism. But it is not an uncommon assumption: that autistic people just don't care.

I first heard of autism about twenty-five years ago. I have never forgotten it. There was a TV documentary of some kind, filmed inside the house of the family of a boy with autism, who was perhaps about eight or nine years old. The house, or the room that was being filmed at least, was in a state of disrepair and untidiness, which was attributed to the boy's destructive behaviour. Included in the film was footage of the boy banging his head against the wall of the room. His mother subsequently spoke to camera about the frequency of that behaviour, and about how upsetting she found it.

Whether or not the boy's mother or the film's narrator offered this explanation for the boy's troubling behaviour, I cannot recall, but I clearly remember coming away from this, my first exposure to autism, with the idea that autistic children so little care about other people, even about members of their immediate family, that they often act so as to distress them, as a way of punishing them or 'getting at' them or something of that kind. So persuaded was I by this idea of autism that on more than one occasion during the years that followed, before ever I had children of my own, I observed in conversation that a thing that I would wish to avoid more than anything was to become the mother of a child with autism. Because, according to my understanding during all of that time, a child with autism is a child who cannot care, who bangs his head against your sitting room wall just because he knows that you cannot stand it.

I was wrong about all of that. For one thing, an autistic child is simply not capable of the kind of circuitous thinking and acting that would be involved in choosing to bang their head as a way of getting at you; there is a quite magnetic directness about young people with autism, a guilelessness, an innocence, and it derives precisely from their inability to calculate in this way. So, the boy on the documentary from twenty-five years ago was not punishing his mother with a behaviour that he calculated would be most upsetting to her. The reason that he was banging his head was much more likely to have been an unbearable load of stimulation, to be fended off only by the kind of deep and distracting pressure that is produced by walking on tip-toes, by spinning around, by squeezing into tight spaces and, yes, unfortunately, by banging your head against a wall. The fact that his mother would naturally intervene every time he banged his head against the wall, as she would not, say, when he walked on his toes, is relevant, but not as proof of his uncaring manipulation of his mother's feelings. In a world in which few interactions are negotiable by you, in a world whose filtering of sensory input simply does not work for you, in a world in which you must bear the load of almost infinitely incomprehensible stimulation, any interaction which you can generate that is predictable and makes sense is, obviously, one to which you are drawn, even at the price of bruising and pain. The boy's mother reached once again for his head to hold it, just as he knew she would, and that ease, of being held, of knowing that he would be held and of being held, was shelter in his autistic storm.

Children with autism do care. In fact, given the importance for them of stability and familiarity, they care even more than you and I do. If you are a person in their life, then you are likely bigger and more beautiful to them than they can ever be to you – that is their nature.

The first time that I left Joseph during his autistic life was when he was about four-and-a-half years old. He was still almost wholly non-verbal, able to produce a word like 'book,' perhaps, but only rarely and never in a reciprocal context. For some months, we had been using the

'Picture Exchange Communication System' with him, with some effect. He had begun to be able to build up the simple sentence, 'I want – book/jigsaw/chocolate – please' using three pictures placed along a velcro strip ('I want' 'book' 'please'). Joseph was even beginning to be able to read this sentence once he had put it together, thus approximating a conventional request for his book or his jigsaw, which were out of reach but visible so as to motivate the communication. Joseph also had a book of polaroid photographs of his family and a few family friends and significant places, again to encourage him to share the fact that he was thinking about them when to do so with spoken language was – still mostly is – quite beyond him.

Very shortly after my return from being away overnight, Joseph put together a sentence on his velcro strip. It was the first time that he had done something like this, and he never repeated it. He brought the sentence to his dad. On it was the symbol for 'I want' and the symbol for 'please.' In between was the polaroid picture of me. And what is more, in his stilted wooden voice, so lacking in intonation, so robotic, so apparently 'unfeeling,' this little boy who could not talk, with an effort of concentration that we can never approximate, managed to say, 'I want – Mama – please.' Why? I suppose that he had cared very much that I had not been there.

It was an unforgettable moment. But it was not the moment when I discovered that Joseph could care. Of this, I had never been in doubt. He had never used language to say so, of course – nor has he since. He had never produced the conventional hug or kiss – nor has he since. Yet no one who has seen Joseph sidle up to me and to others in his life, and rub against us with his whole body, and stare – really stare – up into our face, and grin, teeth gritted with force of feeling – no one who has seen this could be in any doubt that Joseph really cares. But he cares, as we all should know that we must, with his touch, with his skin, squeezing into that tight space behind you on the chair, too close for signal, too close for anything but comfort.

The very idea that at some time in the future Joseph might number among his peers, piling into their classroom on a Monday morning. The idea, that he might greet his teacher – probably one of the most loved people in his life – with 'Hi Miss, how was your weekend?' The idea! The effort it will be for Joseph to produce the phrase, if he ever does manage such a thing. The concentration, the force of will, to signal conventionally along with all the rest. The amount he will have to care, just to trump his native inability – an amount of care so expended in the effort of finding and producing words that tone and expression will not be attained. Not one of his fellow students will care as much as Joseph does that morning – not specifically about your weekend, perhaps, but about you. He will care about you.

Joseph may never succeed at this kind of conventional signalling. Many people with autism find it difficult, sometimes impossible, to use language in that way. Especially at times when the stakes are high. Commenting upon the world is one thing. But when something needs to be said ('I want toilet please,' 'I want help please') or when another person is in play ('How are you?' 'What is your name?') – these are situations in which autistic people experience such intensity, in which *they care so much*, that they just cannot find the words.

Why is it that autistics find themselves lost for words in this way? Just when they need most, just when they want most, just when they care most? Is it because speaking requires indifference? Because language presupposes a kind of carelessness? A certain distance from what is going on? Like all signals, do words work well only when you are standing well back, removed from goings on and not awash with the world? Is it this indifference, this carelessness, this distance, that the autistic child is incapable of? Michel Serres tells a story of being stung in the thigh by a hornet while giving a public lecture. He reports having carried on speaking regardless, and speculates that, had ne not been speaking, had he been smelling a flower or climbing a rock face, he would have been overwhelmed by the pain. Speaking, Serres says, anaesthetizes our bodies, language dialling back the intensity of our experience.

It is one of the many ironies of autism that the tone in which autistics speak, if they do speak, seems so flat, so affectless, so uncaring. They have had to overcome their native excess of affection, their defining abundance of care, in order to speak! For, the most ubiquitous set of signals of them all – spoken language – requires and produces the same distance from the world and one another that all signals require and produce, a distance that those with autism either cannot achieve or, if they manage to achieve it, painfully testify to in the flatness of their intonation and the inexpressiveness of their speaking faces. If they cared less, they could speak more…more easily, more carelessly.

How many of those other students, trooping into their classroom on that Monday morning and casually – with just the right expression, which comes so naturally to them – pronounce, 'Hi Miss, how was your weekend?' – how many of those other students to whom this so offhand of signals comes so readily – how many of them care about your weekend? Is not 'Hi Miss, how was your weekend?' just the same as all those other 'Hi, how are you?'s that we fling about the place without a second or a first thought? How often are they answered? And how surprised we are, how taken aback, how awakened from our slumbers, when someone answers something other than, 'Fine, how was yours?', or 'Good, thanks, how are you?' These bandyings are so often the mere substitutes for care, polished markers of just the right texture that they flow off the oiled surface of our interactions. Signals, where care might be but is not.

But the one with autism cannot signal, or cannot do it well. Because the one with autism cannot not care. In fact, to produce a version of the signal – to pass muster – she will have to care so much that she will exhaust her resources in the effort, and never really pass muster, never really achieve that blasé carelessness of the word-signals that trip so easily off our tongues.

Temple Grandin is an autistic person who gives talks on autism all over the world – delivered in an uneven tone and looping around the salient points, because she cannot really pass muster either. She describes having spoken in Silicon Valley to a group of parents of children with autism. During the session, she was asked by one parent – 'How do we know that our children care about us?' To this she replied, 'If your house is on fire, they will help you get out.'

But that is not enough for us, sufferers from Autistic Society Disorder. We are not satisfied by care. We want to see that we care. We want signals of care. And in the proper tone. With just the right show of feeling.

*

Our Autistic Society Disorder has been the death of care. By its nature indistinct, in-common and diffusely circulating, care is choked of air by the categorizing, organizing, managing and manipulating effects of ASD, which seeks to enclose our relations with ourselves, the world and other people, to render them rigidly predictable and to block the vitality that they would circulate between them. And yet, care might have made us immune to ASD, comprising as it does those very achievements of indistinctness and circulation that would prevent ASD from taking hold. The battle between ASD and care was, for this reason, longer and more fraught than the battles between ASD and education and health. But care did succumb in the end. Our autistic society did at last contain that which might have protected us from its ills.

Two centuries ago, when our institutions of education and health began to be established, care was so obviously anathema that we shied away for a while from attempts to simulate it. It sufficed merely to oversee the dissolution of pre-industrial forms, by which care was quietly traded within households and in communities in a manner constitutive of their fabric, by which care made part of the commons – those unregulated, diffuse resources that are now under watchful lock and key.

In time to nurture a stronger, longer-lived workforce, and in time to assuage lobbying against the atrocity of industrial living conditions, early hesitation in instituting care at last came to an end. Care was officially admitted, on condition of its close confinement within the walls of a new institution, a soft institution unlike those of health and education: the institution of the *home*.

For all that we are now used to regarding the home as a space that is natural to human life, the home is an invention of the nineteenth century. People before then had roofs over their head, of course. People prepared food and slept soundly and gave birth and died away. But all of this was done in spaces quite unlike the enclosed, specialized, cordoned off, curtained in, home of the Victorian era. As late as the early nineteenth century, even large and rich houses were built to contain relatively few rooms, with huge windows and doors, and wide casements and balconies; their inhabitants enjoyed a mixed-economy life that was outward looking, public. It took the beginnings of the effort to institutionalize care for the home as we know it to emerge, a domestic space for the simultaneous exercise and containment of care, staffed by a new kind of worker, another invention of the institutional age: the homemaker – a woman, shadow of her former self, whose life was destined for the very first time to remain systematically unseen.

It was with tremendous caution that care entered our institutional society, curtailed to the margins of effort and enterprise, unsignalled inevitably, for care does not admit of signal, without price or wage, indistinct still, but stripped of its other essential aspect – for care had ceased to circulate, kept within the walls of the purpose-built family home.

Only once care could be safely let out again, under the rigid conditions of an autistic society – only once care could be rendered distinct, that is, made subject to the criteria and strategies and regulations and assessments that are the other side of the coins of price and wage – did the home begin to be established in a more visibly institutional way. Care once again ventured out of doors, but it no longer circulated freely and was no longer indistinct. The care of children, old people and those with special needs was gradually accorded its price – the lowest of prices, of course, for care is still potentially the gravest threat to ASD. And so appeared the *care home*, an institution that rendered care distinct, open to measurement and monetization, and that, in doing so, sounded the death knell of care.

The *care home:* staffed almost exclusively by women, who trade duties of care in their own home for duties of care in a more explicitly institutional home. These women – these *carers* – use care homes to care for their own children and old people in order to care for others' children and old people, who have traded being cared for by the unseen and unpaid work of women in their family for being cared for by the hardly seen and hardly paid work of women they have never met. The *care home*, and its more recent underbelly *home care*, which has seen the newly-distinct duties of care re-enter the home that had incubated them for so long, completing the circle of non-care to which care has been consigned by our society, so that those women who might have cared for their own families in their own homes, indistinctly though contained, instead care for other women's families in other women's homes, distinctly and still contained. The pushing around of care between women in the shadows or just out of the shadows of life and work, a low-temperature laundering of the life of care by women who increasingly don't care.

Of course, they don't care – how could they? They do not know your old father and mother. They do not know your small baby. Drawn from the ranks of the most disadvantaged and signalled as all but worthless, they must simulate an effect – care – to which the institution in which they work is anathema. A 2018 survey by University College London, which questioned the staff of care homes all across the UK, found that there is abuse and neglect in nine out of ten of them. No surprise. A study from ten years before found that half of those working in care homes in the US made use of food banks to feed themselves and their families. These women are tired. They are hungry. They miss their parents and children and are expected to care for the parents and children of others. Of course, they neglect and abuse. Just as most women do in their situation.

Shortly after I gave birth for the first time, I received a communication from the UK National Health Service – a leaflet on steps to take if you felt the impulse to shake your baby. I tossed it away. Shake my baby? Shake that tiny, sleeping being, so reliant, so sweet? But a baby does not always sleep and is not always sweet. After weeks of colic and crying in a home to which nobody came during the day, I experienced the impulse to shake my baby, from frustration and exhaustion and a loss of any sense of connection with a world in which the normal rules apply. I think that many new mothers experience this, confined to a home whose carceral effect is so belied by its advertisement as a place of comfort and care that you have not even the consolation of resenting your prison but must look to yourself to explain the temptation to abuse and neglect.

New mothers are not vindictive any more than care workers are. But when you are installed in institutions of care that actively annihilate the possibility of care while demanding that you simulate care in the shadows of life – that will make an abuser out of anyone.

Care is abused in the home. Care is neglected in the home. Because the home strangles care's vital components: circulation and indistinctness; commonness and immeasurableness. In the home, care, which can only run free, undergoes its double containment.

There is a care home close to where I live, pleasantly secluded behind a line of old oak trees. On its cut-stone outer wall hangs a banner, on which is printed 'All the ingredients needed for a perfect care home.' The text is illustrated by a computer-generated image in brown and blue, of a 1950s-style armchair (brown) with a cushion and arm-protectors (blue), placed on top of a small circular floor-mat (blue) and next to an occasional table (brown) on which rests a teacup and saucer (blue) and which is lit by a standard lamp (brown) with a fabric shade (blue). A more generic image one could hardly devise – the kind of thing that some marketing intern might have rustled up on her first day, riffing lazily on the theme of 'old person.'

This banner, with its bold assertion and simplistic cartoon, captures the active eradication of care that is the essence of the care home. Care – real care – is not comprised of 'ingredients' that can be listed out and ticked off, arranged in a recipe to be followed by anyone or by no-one in a mindless, heartless administration of the aged and otherwise vulnerable. Old people and young children and those with disabilities are not generic types, to be summarized by the smooth lines and simple tones of stock images and standard routines. And insofar as they require care, what they require is just the opposite of what is promised by the care home's glossy advertisement: interaction that is low-key and constant, up close and personal, with no ingredients and no recipe. What they require is the opposite of ASD: the easy reciprocity that comes of the judgement born of experience, and the modest constancy that has neither clear boundary nor clean line.

The signals of care – care's garish display – are becoming more generic and lazy the more we look for them and not for care. *Hello Lovelies!*, from your media monopolist. *We care about your experience with us*, from your banking corporation. And *Aw, bless*! from your barely-there mother, reacting to the antics of her child while keeping a firm eye or two on her phone. Behind these simplistic signals, care ceases to circulate, chilled by the cold neglect of these as-if warm, as-if caring displays. The media company that declares how lovely you are leaves you waiting on the phone for an hour, the bank that cares so much about your experience refuses to serve your 'everyday banking needs,' and the absent-without-leave mother, well...

One morning during the first few weeks of Joseph's schooling, I overheard the mother of one of his classmates speaking to a friend about the distress of her young son as he was being brought to school every morning. 'I don't know where this is coming from,' she said. 'I mean, he's been at nursery since he was six months.' Presumably, the mother's reasoning was that a boy of four-and-a-half years old, who has known nothing but institutional life, ought to be accustomed to institutions and not really care when he is dropped off to spend the day at a new one. But when we consider the premises of this common brand of reasoning, it is revealed as truly chilling.

A young baby, having established a reliance on the presence of his mother for the first six months of his life, a reliance relatively undiluted by receptivity to the world – an almost absolute reliance and an urgently existential one – is suddenly consigned to the care of people whom he has never met, whose smell and tone and touch is entirely unfamiliar and who, no matter how kind, do not know him and do not care about him. During the next four years, the small boy encounters many new people whose job it is to 'care' for him, his awareness dawning in tandem with an anxious watchfulness that the person who was there for him yesterday is the person who will be there for him today – the poor remuneration of carers riddles their job with precariousness. And still, through the repeated ravages of these affectionate hopes, still he has managed to wring from his pre-school institution some modicum of care, to which he has attached himself much more tenaciously than if the modicum were more fulsome and more reliable. When it is crumbs you have to eat, you are more jealous of them than is the rich man of the feast spread out before him.

And then, having sustained his little heart through it all, he is ridiculed by his own mother for not wishing to exchange one institution for another, for not blithely relinquishing his little crumb of care – for still, despite it all, having kept on caring.

Early accounts of autism blamed the condition on the mothers of those affected. Mothers were suspected of being so uncaring as to have made their offspring autistic. Prisoners in their homes, consigned to fulfill all alone and in the shadows the work of care that ought to range freely in community, these women were accused of shirking their invisible work, of not caring enough, of being cold. Refrigerator Mothers, they were called. The theory is no longer a popular one. And yet, a version of it may require revival. For the autistic society in which we now live is a Refrigerator Society in which everything that would circulate between us is petrified. And a Refrigerator Society makes Refrigerator Mothers of us all.

*

With the institutionalization of care, Autistic Society Disorder reaches the culmination of our remaking as compatible with the social, political and economic world order: recast, by institutions of health, as beings who have traded our body for a quasi-medical soul, the repository of a generic truth about our specific selves; readied, by institutions of education, as beings sufficiently removed from reality to be the unwitting reproducers of engineered realities; and restricted, by institutions of care, as beings so at risk from sublime threat that only an explicit gesture of salvation can, at any moment, be meaningful and sufficient, to the detriment of human interconnection.

Just as the institutions of health have blocked our interaction with what we should feel within ourselves, with their *labels* and the truth they seem to promise; and just as the institutions of education have blocked our interaction with the world around us, with their *concepts* and the reality they seem to constitute; so the institutions of care have blocked our interaction with one another, with their *signals* and the virtue they seem to indicate.

It is blockage, then, that is the main business of our institutions. Blockage of our connections with ourselves, the world and other people. These connections are channeled through ever proliferating labels, concepts and signals, whose rigidity is the enemy of any but the most generic and predictable of meanings, strangling those experiences that would circulate indistinctly in living, breathing human cultures. Indeed, indistinctness and circulation, traits that are essential to care, are the main targets of Autistic Society Disorder, not only in its institutions of care but also in its institutions of health and education. After all, it is not only our love for one another that must circulate indistinctly. That for which so-called health and so-called education substitute – living and learning – are also, by their nature, indistinct and circulating, to be taken for granted, implied, rather than rendered explicit and managed. In fact, in their meaningful forms, education, health and care are even indistinct from one another, circulating between themselves such that their being enshrined in separate institutions itself does violence to their character as diffuse and organically traded. Let us have education over here and health over here and care over here is an originary violence, a first blocking of the meaningful interaction – with ourselves, the world and other people – a first refrigeration of energies that did and that ought to run free.

What else is that *involvement* that is set at naught by the step back and look of our institutions of education, than caring about what is put before us or taught to us as we would do if we did our learning in contexts native to a way of life? We do not call it 'education' when we learn how to angle our foot so that a ball that it strikes will curve through the air because we likely care very much as we learn it. And what else is that refusal of labels which the autistic person, like all people, requires in order to thrive – in order to *feel fine*, which is the one condition that goes without a label of our institutions of health – what else is this than the implicit, unnoticed, ability to care about things, that is, to get on with our lives? We know that we are returning to health when we begin to care about our usual routines once again.

Far from being available for the distinctions – the labels, the concepts, the signals – that are the currency of our institutions, the learning, living and loving for which we sadly substitute education, health and care are not even distinguishable from each other. When we do care about what is going on, we learn; when we can care about what is going on, we are alive; when we care and are cared for, we love and are loved. All, in the end, is care. And care is the absence of ASD.

Polar Institutions

5

Society

A man describes the strategy adopted by himself and his wife, according to which each is assigned a 'Me-Time Pass' that can be activated with a minimum of a half-hour's notice and that allows for household chores, care of children, and other duties to be dropped in favour of 'Me-Time' – exercise, online shopping, something of that kind. The man seems triumphant in the arrangement, recommending it to his friend as bringing an end to conjugal bickering.

What model of relationship is this? Might a cohabiting couple not trust each other to act for the good of themselves and their family? Might they not discern tiredness in one another and take over arduous duties for a while? Might they not endure their daily tasks in spite of exhaustion so as to avoid causing annoyance or inconvenience? Apparently not. But why not? What is the blockage in this man's relations with his partner from which the Me-Time Pass presents a triumphant release? What has happened to the reciprocity that might constitute their living together, that they must strategize a reciprocity-effect?

To summarize autism in a single phrase, one might describe it as the opposite of reciprocity, as the inability – great or small – to enter into reciprocal relations. If

Joseph is asked to wave at someone, he waves with the palm of his hand facing towards himself. That is what he observes when people wave to him; the palm of their hand faces towards him. And so he replicates their wave but without that ingredient of reciprocity that so effortlessly, so naturally it seems, turns our palm towards the other person. We might judge, for this reason, that it is the absence of a fundamental, and otherwise apparently natural, reciprocity that constitutes the essence of being autistic. When Joseph falls and hurts himself, when he hits his head off the corner of the table or drops something heavy onto his toes, he cries, yes, but he does not look to anyone for help or comfort. Rubbing his hands on his bruised forehead and sobbing with the shock and the pain, it does not occur to him that there might be someone nearby whose ministrations might console. It is something that he must be taught – when he hurts himself, I rush to hug him so that the opportunity is not lost to form with him the habit of seeking support in times of stress.

It is not unlikely that only exposure to autism's want of reciprocity shows up just how reciprocal our relations generally are; reciprocity is so fundamental that we tend to take it for granted. We are familiar, for instance, with the halting attempts at question and answer made by the very young but we may never have considered that the seemingly natural bond between question and answer does not necessarily obtain. Never, that is, until we encounter a young person with autism: who may be able to name an object – 'book'; who may even be able to read the sentence – 'That is a book'; but who, when asked, 'What is that?' by someone who is holding a book in front of her, is likely to falter. She can say the word 'book,' she can read the word 'book,' but she cannot answer with the word 'book.' At most, she may manage to repeat the question – 'What is that?' – replicating in her effort at dialogue what she achieves in her effort at a wave, answering with the question that was asked of her.

Even a question about themselves – about something that they would like to eat or do – is just too hot for the child with autism to handle. 'Joseph, would you like some chocolate?' must be followed by the Makaton sign for 'yes' if Joseph is to be able to answer that he does. At present, I am teaching him how to reply to the question, 'How are you?'. We have made some progress. I have taught him that the answer is 'Good, thank you' – there can only be a stock answer, a strategic move to survive the conversation. Now, when I ask, 'Joseph, how are you?' – loud and clear, with my whole being framing the fact that we are practicing our answer and with the Makaton signs for support – Joseph replies: first, 'How are you?,' and then if I give him time, 'Good, thank you.' A rudimentary echo of basic reciprocity, acquired with great effort as a strategy to make it through, learnt off by heart like the nine times tables. As for *asking* a question – 'Hi Miss, how was your weekend?': for the moment at least, that is a world away.

Yet these are such simple reciprocities, about such immediate effects. Think of more complex ones, the glancing observation of a frown, perhaps, and the recalibration of tone and gesture so as to be more conciliatory. Think of all the arts of our interactions, the give-and-take of our relations, their push-and-pull, their warp-and-woof, the intricate weave of our ways of living together. Into these ways of living the child with autism seems unable to enter; to him, they appear to be mysterious and exclusive. But are they in fact growing mysterious to us all? Are strategies coming so universally to substitute for reciprocities that the dance of our interactions is being gradually broken down, into easy steps convenient for administering and adjusting? Are we all now growing autistic? What else can explain why two people who live together no longer interpret and alleviate their mutual exhaustion but cling instead to their Me-Time Pass, an entirely rigid substitute for expressions of dispiritedness, which produces every time its stock response: within a half-hour the other person steps in to look after the children as predictably and as well as Joseph will eventually reply, 'Good, thank you,' when someone is minded to ask him, 'How are you?'

What is it that readies two people who live together to live together like this? What has dissolved the complementarity of their coexistence that they apply such strategies to mediate between them? What has unpicked the threads of their relations so as to launder them through explicit benefits – Me-Time – that are to be evenly distributed? The answer brings us to the polar institutions of our time, which together constitute the platform on which is staged an endless circulation of the labels, concepts and signals of health, education and care: the two poles of our increasingly autistic world, which, between them, flatten the rise and fall of our relations, rendering them thin and poor of meaning and vulnerable at every point to interference and rearrangement.

The first of these institutions is what we call 'Society,' and its defining effect is to activate the labels and concepts and signals of health, education and care with the *strategies* that bring them to life…or, at least, to what passes for life once our ways of life have been dismantled. Relations between our man and his wife, like so many of our relations with one another now, are *social* relations, and *social* relations are those in which reciprocities are replaced by strategies so that our ways of living together grow more rigid and more meaningless, which is to say, more autistic, every day.

It is not what we are usually told: that to be social is to be autistic. In fact, we are usually told the opposite: that to be autistic is to be not, or not very, social. Yet, insofar as our relations with one another are growing as rigid and poor as those between the man and his wife with their Me-Time Pass; and insofar as such strategies are made available to us on the social sites to which we apply and which we negotiate almost constantly; and insofar as autism is a condition requiring even the most basic interrelation to be made explicit and then strategic: what else can we conclude than that to be social is to be autistic?

But this means that what makes a child stand out in a manner to attract a diagnosis of autism is not, after all, an abnormal reliance on social strategies but, in fact, an abnormal resistance to social strategies; you are labelled 'autistic' – and more and more young people are labelled 'autistic' – if you cannot, or cannot easily, acquire the social skills necessary to identify and apply appropriate strategies for interaction. That all we have to help these young people are more strategies to compensate for their lack of affinity with strategies is their, and our, great tragedy. For, children with autism are the canaries in our coalmine, struggling with all of their might against the grain of our Society, crying out to those who might listen against the erosion of ways of living in which reciprocity is natural by the encroachment of social life in which reciprocity is strategic.

*

An example: In response to students' concerns that they are not being facilitated in efforts to compensate for missing class, their lecturer sends them an email detailing ways in which students can access material from classes they are unable to attend. Among these ways is listed one 'strategy,' that of 'asking a friend' for their notes from the class or their verbal summary of its content.

The strategy of asking a friend: the easy reciprocity of student friendship, apparently not available but compensated for by an institutionally approved strategy for producing a friendship-effect. One thin strand of student life: separated out, laundered through the institution, and returned with full institutional support but without the life because stripped of its connection to any other strand of student life. Once this is achieved with a sufficient number of strands of student life, student life is left threadbare, the lifeless strands all that remain as a limp consolation. No unplanned afternoons drinking beer in the sun – debating ideas just encountered, maybe – only #beerinthesun afternoons, sponsored by a local brewery; no first-day friend from the queue to register for your subject, only the Student-Buddy assigned to you by the Mentoring System. Everything you desire just as you desire it, only too explicit, too planned, too strategic for life.

Yet these students have so very many friends that we might imagine them to be adept at friendship and in no need whatsoever of *the strategy of asking a friend.* Those who use the social media site, Facebook, for instance, have an average of three hundred and thirty-eight friends. But all or almost all of these friends are made via channels mapped out by the Facebook site, and all or almost all of them adopt Facebook strategies – you post an image of your new dress and your friends automatically return with a stock response, variations on 'Wow' probably, or, most stock of all stock responses, a click on the 'Like' button, complete with its Makaton sign. Consider Joseph's struggle to learn to reply 'Good, thank you' to the question 'How are you?'. Then consider the average Facebook user – who has as yet no diagnosis of autism – immediately responding with 'Like' to everything from cupcakes to job promotions to the death of a grandmother to support for Black Lives Matter. Little wonder that asking a friend for notes from a missed lecture must be recast as a strategy framed and recommended by an institution – friendship is fast becoming nothing but a set of strategies, its gestures selected from a drop-down list of ready-made options, less and less reliant upon our active participation but shivering through us as we mouth its script and push its buttons.

The reciprocities that allow us to live with one another are thus gradually replaced by the strategies that allow us to *cope* with one another. Three-hundred and thirty-eight, after all, is a vast number of friends. In the Victorian novels, of Dickens for example, characters are often described as having *a friend*. One friend. Are we such masters of friendship that we can maintain three hundred and thirty-eight? Think of the complex arts of friendship: the sympathy and the judgment, the commonalities and the compromises – how is it possible to negotiate these pleasures and pains with three hundred and thirty-eight? It is not possible, for even the most virtuosic of friends. Which is why the arts of friendship are now so willingly relinquished in favour of ready-made protocols that allow us to manage what might otherwise overwhelm. Just select a response from the stock of unobjectionable options – no need even to learn it off like the nine times tables – and another onslaught of friendship is *dealt with*, albeit in fairly rigid style and with possibilities for meaning reduced to having, simply, responded something rather than nothing, and with each friend recast as a cypher for strategies of friendship rather than a living breathing being to have and to hold.

And it is not only friendship that requires to be thus dealt with – even more intimate relations are now remade as social, their previously woven strands separated out, rendered explicit, and rearranged into organized possibilities for association. Our man with his Me-Time Pass affords a chilling glimpse into the conversion of conjugal relations into strategic arrangements, which are thick now with the likes of 'Dad Days' and 'Date Nights,' and which I have witnessed being administered remotely via a diary stored on each person's phone. More startling still: the transformation of the relation between a mother and her baby into a set of management procedures. 'Parenting' is the umbrella term for these procedures, a coarse designator that changes what might have been a stalwart frontier of reciprocity into a strategic arrangement through and through. Indeed, perhaps no other relation is so plainly named as one that is to be *coped with* than the relation between a mother and her offspring – 'How was your weekend?' so often answered by a wry look and, 'We *managed*.' Hence the bustling industry of

119

parenting guides: use the word 'no' only three times a day, or once a day, or not at all; hug twice at bedtime but not if she wakes during the night; make eye contact when you are pleased but not when you are displeased...So many strategies, which constitute and negotiate a set of interactions that are still advertised as somehow natural or instinctive. So many strategies, to forestall a mother and her young baby from *rubbing along together*, as the saying expressively goes; in fact, that embodied possibility – of rubbing along together – must now expend itself in the anxiety-laden urgency of 'skin to skin' just after birth, itself, of course, a parenting strategy, a strand of previous reciprocities, separated out, simplified, and assigned to its rightful time and place. Skin to skin: offering to the newly born the briefest of interfaces between the reciprocity of pre-partum existence and the strategy of all that is to follow.

It is no surprise, after all: our craving for management suggestions; no surprise that our inboxes are crammed with invitations to training courses on which we will be taught newer and better strategies for dealing with the social situations that, it seems to our hearts as they ice over, multiply exponentially. How to manage difficult colleagues at work. How to make an impact as an introvert. How to drive inclusion and engagement. How to introduce yourself to create a confident impression. How to have courageous conversations. Tactics for responding assertively to verbal challenges. Strategies for asking a friend. Ways of making time for you in your marriage. Techniques for bonding with your baby. As the last remaining configurations of our existence crumble to irrelevance, the social is revealed as a black hole into which all our ways of living have disappeared; every aspect of our relations with one another, remade as strategic. 'It's good to move to a neighbourhood where people know how be new,' a woman once told me. Welcoming your neighbour, talking to your wife, asking your friend, holding your newborn…not a stone of our relations left unturned, not a moment of would-be reciprocity left un-strategized beyond the last lingering inch of would-be life.

And the irony is, once the foundation stones of our relations have been turned strategic then our relations require strategies to be endured. Without a strategy, they are overwhelming. Without a strategy, they are an assault. Neighbours, an assault. Wives, an assault. Friends, an assault. Newborns, an assault. Each one an eruption of would-be three-dimensional existence, an invasion of our two-dimensional world, requiring a strategy to be appropriately flattened down. We log onto Facebook and the assault is immense: three hundred and thirty-eight friends, already almost entirely flattened by Facebook, of course, but still with the air of three dimensions about them – like nestlings, beaks open, demanding to be fed. Small wonder that we cleave to the strategies; small wonder that we move our cursor to the drop-down list and suppress our dwindling capacity for human sympathy with our ever-growing habit of *dealing with* one another. And when we do happen upon a single friend – a neighbour walking down our street, perhaps – far from offering some relief they tend rather to partake of the smothering character of all our interactions; so traumatized are we by our three hundred and thirty-eight that even a single friend, one friend, is, for us, an assault and must be reduced, via the tritest of talk, to the two dimensional.

If one *lives* reciprocities one aims only to *survive* with the strategies that replace them. And the value of surviving comes quietly to exceed the value of living, as we lose our appreciation for the complex nuances of life in our constantly refreshed relief at survival solutions. This undoubtedly explains our recent, wholesale and willing, adoption of platforms like Zoom, which distil the essence of our social interactions. All of a sudden – literally from nowhere – we are in the 'presence' of another person, or three other people, or twenty other people. Truly, an assault. Truly, the would-be three-dimensional invading two-dimensional space. Truly, an ordeal that must be got through, survived. But the strategies are included in the package; entirely strategic possibilities for interaction come complete with the 'tools' to realise them: how to mute other people; how to optimize your background; how to touch up your appearance…how to insert your questions and time your answers. These social platforms have done what, previously, only autism has appeared to do, what previously we might not have imagined could be done:

with their pixilated lag, they have severed the question from its answer, unpicked the rhythm of question and answer, and substituted for it their strategies for question and answer, strategies that extend to the content and the timing of question and answer. My question no longer courts your answer; my answer is hardly a response to your question – my question is asked according to strategies for questioning; your answer is given according to strategies for answering. There is my question and there is your answer, and never the twain shall meet outside of rigid solutions very poor of meaning. Human interaction, broken down to its component parts then fixed up with strategies devised to reconnect them.

The social is a pincer move against reciprocity. It mediates our interactions, gets into them, separates them out. And then it mediates between them, connects them, brings them together. It ruptures and it sutures, breaks reciprocities and galvanises with strategies. The dance of our interactions reconstructed but without its flow, without its feel, without its life.

Joseph has life enough, often more than his typical peers. But he does not have life in conversation. In conversation, when he is not distressed, he is deadened, eyes staring into the distance, voice quiet and flat. Yet are we not deadened too, in our Zoom-style interactions? Are we not the living dead? Eyes open but no peripheral vision. Eyes open but looking at no-one. Eyes open, like those of a corpse. Everything of life, suppressed.

Everything human, filtered out. Everything bodied, screened off.

At the beginning of its 2020 'lockdown,' the UK government called for volunteers to offer help to those who might need it in the weeks ahead – those living alone, those with infirmities, the old, the vulnerable. The call was immediately answered by seven-hundred-and-fifty thousand people, all with the urge to be a friend to their neighbour but with simply no idea of how to do it. Devising strategies for it at short notice was not the priority and so reports began to trickle out, of the frustration and disillusionment of the volunteers, almost none of whom was employed in any way. The impulse remains, then, if only as species memory: the urge to associate with one another, to help one another, to live – really live - together. But the urge lacks established pathways of expression, familiar and embedded outlets to make it effective, to give it meaning. Suspended in thin air, it grows weaker and gasps for breath, and travels more and more unresistingly along the lifeless channels set up for it.

How many of those untasked volunteer helpers – how many of the expectant three-quarters of a million, waiting patiently for their friendship assignment – at last spent their drive to offer support to their neighbour in the hastily cobbled strategy of Clapping for Carers, standing outside their homes every Thursday evening at eight o'clock, squandering their hopes of living together in a meaningful way in another generic and entirely ineffective strategy. Such reversals of fortune in our would-be reciprocal relations, such headings-off of our vestiges of community spirit, do act upon us in the end, sucking the life from our urge to really live together and rendering us as passive applicants to social strategies, which pass through our wasted bodies almost without our volition.

Meanwhile, after twelve weeks of 'lockdown,' seven-hundred people in London were reported as having died alone in their home, with no one for company as the curtain fell on their lonely life, with no one even to notice that they were gone. What tiny happenstance, what by-the-way contingency, at last raised the alarm on these friendless souls? – some of the vast fallout from the essential indifference, the assault upon reciprocity, that is our social, our autistic, style of life.

*

There is the danger that appeals to reciprocity are heard as wishful hearkening after some imagined pre-industrial utopia; how often now are concrete suggestions of deterioration in our lives dismissed as misguided nostalgia. But describing the element of reciprocity is neither utopian nor misguided, designating no more and no less than those embedded forms of interaction that have characterized, and still characterize, fulsomely established ways of life. These forms of interaction are not, in their reciprocity, assumed to be 'equal' or 'fair.'

On the contrary, very often they enshrine stark imbalances, in the burden of labour, for example, or the division of property. But these imbalances are part of an arrangement, a reciprocal arrangement, woven into a way of life, and are not therefore to be separated out and established as discrete phenomena available for strategic review.

A newsletter from my vegetable-box scheme tells of improvements to farm practices east of Kampala in Uganda. Twenty years ago, so the newsletter reports, there was not much 'gender equality' there: the women did most of the tending of crops and the men did most of the talking and drinking. Since then, it claims, the charity Send A Cow has worked with locals, providing them with agricultural training once they have addressed their 'gender issues.' Now, we are told, the men and women east of Kampala are embracing a fairer and more productive division of tasks.

Twenty years ago, the way of life east of Kampala assigned to women the task of tending the crops and to men that of talking together while drinking. To our Western eyes, this looks like exploitation. Why should only the women tend the crops? we ask. This must change, we say. Existing arrangements must be broken down and rearranged such that the pains and the pleasures of tending and talking are distributed evenly. But our interpretation of arrangements of reciprocity as exploitative is an imposition of our *social* styles onto where they are neither native nor appropriate, a dissolution of carefully balanced ecosystems of reciprocities in favour of the level-playing field of Society that we know and think we love. Why should only the women tend the crops? we ask, unaware of the tacit aggressions in our question. For one thing, why do we not ask why only the men should do the talking? Why is talking more desirable than tending the crops? Our cursory assessments impose a post-industrial denigration of physical labour. But that is just the start of it. For, our taxonomies, generated by the dismantling of our ways of life, are so crassly unyielding as to inevitably constitute a misapprehension of cultures other than ours.

Were those women east of Kampala really merely 'tending the crops'? For that matter, were those men east of Kampala really merely 'talking'? Ivan Illich describes the densely complex reciprocities characteristic of vernacular cultures of Europe, which are poorly perceived and described by our social categories and expectations. In one valley in the Alps, he tells us, the woman sometimes used the scythe to cut the fodder; but the man always used it to cut the rye. In another valley, only the woman touched the knives in the kitchen. In yet another, both the man and the woman used the knives to cut the bread, but one cut down and away, and the other drew the blade towards the chest. In one place, women fed cows but never the draught animals. Farther east, women milked cows that belonged to the homestead while men milked those in the herd on the manor grounds. The Send A Cow representative, with her category of 'tending the crops,' is ill-equipped even to perceive these regionally embedded reciprocities, delicately balanced and not at all available for analysis according to their 'equality' or 'fairness,' which can only be established once all activities have been rendered discrete and potentially equivalent when refracted through some rough-hewn post-industrial measure.

As for 'talking' – to this very day in Thrace, according to Illich, while the men may be the ones to talk about the dead and their deeds, only the women are allowed to address the dead, to shriek and lament those who have passed away and to invoke their protection. And did the Send A Cow assessor notice what the men were leaning on as they talked, for the Berber man may only lean against the outside of the east wall of his house, the inside walls reserved for leaning against by women.

Why do only the women tend the crops? we ask. There was no answer to that question within the framework of Ugandan culture twenty years ago, not because the set-up there was unreasonable but because the question is unreasonable, riding roughshod over the nuances of a way of life. This way of life, Send A Cow self-righteously rearranged into a 'fairer society,' its representative having been blind to the intricate dance native to the Ugandan territories, seeing nothing but an 'unequal society' and donating her cow only once strategies for producing 'equality' were implemented and reciprocity was no more.

And there is no doubt that the Send A Cow representative is blind to reciprocities wherever she goes. No doubt that, if posted among the people of Ladakh with whom Elena Norberg-Hodge lived for twenty-five years, she would have bemoaned the 'child labour' practices of the locals when she saw the young people of the villages tending the land along with their parents and their grandparents. She would not have seen that there are, or were at least, no 'children' in Ladakh, no people deemed unsuitable for involvement in the life of the community. She would not have seen that the pace of work on the land there was conducted at a rhythm slow enough to be easily undertaken by old and young alike, slow enough to be an occasion for the tacit communication of learning, about slope of land and seasons and crops, slow enough to be inclusive and implicitly resistant to industrial society's constitution of 'children' and 'old people', in part by its imposition of a work-rate premised upon the full expenditure of the energy and strength of a man of twenty years old. The Send A Cow representative would not have seen any of this, with her set of rigid categories and her imperviousness to the reciprocities built into the pace of work and all other aspects of home-spun ways of life, for which our social strategies make an anaemic substitute.

The business of reforming a society in the manner of Send A Cow is really the business of reforming a way of life as a Society, in the process trampling upon delicately established relations of reciprocity. Rituals of living together are broken down into separate components, those components then rendered equivalent and ready for redistribution according to strategies regulated by the abstract concepts that Society brings into play, concepts such as those of 'equality' and 'fairness' and 'friendship' and 'kindness.' This has the effect of extracting the components of ways of living together from the context in which they derive their meaning – nuanced, gendered, seasonal rituals of food production are recast, crudely, as 'tending the crops,' stripped of the details of their regional specificities; the rise and fall of kinds of communication are recast, simply, as 'talking,' tone and content and timing and all other variables, evaporated. These extracted components of ways of life, reduced beyond their native significance, are then subject to a notional and allegedly neutral standard by which they are rendered equivalent – eight hours of tending the crops, say, meriting an hour or two of talking and drinking; even those unsubtle categorizations at last brought under the catch-all pairing of 'work' and 'life,' which, according to procedures of social accounting, must be 'balanced.' Once established in their equivalency, these extracted components of life are then assigned equally to equal actors, with special actors - children, old people, those with disabilities and illnesses – constituted as an ever-growing remainder, requiring off-shoot strategies 'tailored to their special needs' to effect their eventual equivalency to the ever-dwindling standard of the non-special actor.

After this process – of extraction, simplification, and bringing into equivalency of goods, activities and people – there is established a Society, a set-up whose essentially strategic character means that, unlike a closely woven way of life, it is open to readjustment at several points without being in danger of collapse. The 'balance' of 'life' and 'work' may be changed – trialling a four-day working week, for example – and still stability maintained. Policies for a 'more equal' representation of women on the boards of corporations may be introduced – and Society still steady. The place of work may be changed – from office to home, for example – and still no great listing to one side or another. The number of 'friends' required to count as a person of 'influence' may be raised or lowered, and still no fallout. The list of allegiances which automatically debar you from positions of authority may be suddenly altered, and not a ripple ensue. You may even be banned from sitting in the park or seeing your family, and still Society remains on course.

This might be judged a good thing: that we continue to be able to live together despite drastic alterations in our arrangements for living together. In the old fable of the reed and the oak, the oak boasts of its superior substance and strength, yet the reed is proved the longer lasting by its flexibility in high winds. But the story teaches another lesson, quite different from the one most often distilled from it: by shoring up against the prospect of bad storms, by mitigating the risk of uprooting, the reed sacrifices the grandeur, the immensity, the rich and enduring significance of the oak tree, whose shunning of the reed's brand of adaptability is compensated for by its towering stature. A Society that is open to infinite adjustment, which can be tweaked with impunity at a myriad points, is possibly reed-like – thin gruel when compared to the fulsomeness of an established way of life, whose complex reciprocities are not receptive to tinkering with but which, while it remains, provides the kind of consoling support to its people that the infinitely negotiable elements of a Society can never do.

And *support*, in the end, is all: something to lean against, something to rest upon, something to take the pressure off, something to lighten the load.

Our reciprocity-effects are poor, in part because they presuppose that reciprocity is a mode of relation merely between human beings, with no role at all for the rest of the physical world. We are drawn to this presumption by our being steeped in the virtual; Facebook friendship, typical of the reciprocity-effects produced by our social strategies, plays out between human beings so abstracted from the physical world that they are little more than their own avatars, suspended without support from spaces or times or things. Reciprocity between two of such forsaken beings is almost impossible to keep in play – let alone between three hundred and thirty-eight of them; it is as challenging and as tiresome to do so as it would be to keep a ball in the air between them. It is not only the number of friends and the abruptness of their appearances and disappearances that make us abandon efforts to sustain any real reciprocity in favour of the convenience of reciprocity-effects; it is the contextlessness of these friends, their pared-backness to their merely human being, their isolation from the physical world and its supports.

The Berber man leans against the outside of the east wall of his house when he talks to the other men of his community. And he smokes. And he drinks. And the leaning and the smoking and the drinking are supports in his talking, buttresses for it. His interaction with his fellows is propped up. When silence falls, there is smoking to be done, and drinking to be done, and leaning to be done. The reciprocity of the Berber way of life is as much in play between times and places and objects as it is between people. Illich details many such props – the tools of vernacular cultures, their festivals, their crops, their furniture, their food. We may purchase these props in junk shops or bid for them at auctions. His-and-her fireside chairs, for example: his high up with strong armrests, all the better for reading on; hers lower down without armrests, all the better for sewing on. Sexist furniture, we may judge them, contemptuous of their inscription by ways of living; but, seen otherwise, these and so many other of the objects and rituals of meaningful ways of life do as much to support our really living together as do the people who bear a lighter burden as a result.

I have witnessed the last gasps of such embedded reciprocities, refracted through material objects and propped up by times and places. In the kitchen of her farm cottage, my grandmother used to sit by the range cooker, peeling potatoes for dinner. Often, a neighbour would come in; no need for knocking at a door that was always open. A brief greeting, perhaps – 'How are you, Siobhán?' Or maybe just, 'Siobhán.' Then he would stand, leaning back against the kitchen dresser with its crockery display, looking at the range cooker, whose heat, coming from the turf fire within, could absorb the attention, accompany a silent visit, even though the fire was to be heard and smelt but not seen. And my grandmother would continue with the peeling, and the neighbour would continue with the standing, and the reciprocity of their encounter, supported by the potatoes – fine specimens, an improvement on last year's crop – and by the iron stove and by the approach of dinner time, before which the visitor would be leaving…the reciprocity of their encounter did not ask much of them. It was easy. Held in space and in time and by things. A slow dance between the two of them with none of the anxieties that furrow our two-dimensional brows as we attempt to simulate reciprocal relations in thin air.

In our Facebook-style interactions there are no places and no things, no cigarettes for smoking, no wine for drinking, no potatoes for peeling, no fires to soot and spark. It's just you and me – or you and me and three hundred and thirty-six – like a massive job interview, floating in a vacuum, erupting into our day, propped up by nothing. Are we surprised at how suggestible we are in these so-intense encounters, at how ready we are to adopt the recommended strategies? The wall has been dismantled against which we might lean, the rug taken out from under our feet, and we are at a loss. No spaces. No things. No times, even. Dinner no longer approaches. Dinnertime is any time and no time, so that friends might call at any time or at no time. Even the TV schedule has been put out of play, its scant support – 'I can't phone during *East Enders*,' 'Let's call in after the match' – dissipated by 'catch-up' provision, evaporated by the 'record' button. So you can phone at any time, or at no time. And you can call in at any time, or at no time. But if you do phone or if you do call in, be sure not to talk of *East Enders* or of the match; when we no longer share spaces and times and things, we are always potentially trespassing upon those among whom we no longer really live together. The strategies that bring us together have come between us so successfully that we live in constant danger of 'spoiling it' for someone else, and play it much safer by downloading our next move from the social options so readily available.

*

And, counterbalance to our downloading of strategies to determine our social lives is our accompanying uploading of abstract principles to justify our social lives. It is this combination which constitutes the artificial rationality that has displaced the natural feel of ways of life.

What we call 'Society' is founded upon an unfortunate contract, which rechannels arrangements of reciprocity – existing between bodied beings, refracted through material objects, and constituting the ways of a shared world – such that reciprocity flows not between beings but between each being and Society, which henceforth soaks up and manages the reciprocity-requirement of human lives. Society, for this reason, is made up of individual acts carried out for its sake, effecting a laundering of local and contingent reciprocities through a neutral mechanism for the accumulation and redistribution of their social significance. If I sweep the path in front of my house now, it is less and less because my neighbours sweep the path in front of their houses, and more and more because such a show of respect for public throughways is social. Sweeping is abroad in terms of its aggregation rather than its local rationale. It is social to sweep. Conversely, it is anti-social to behave in a manner that, while not necessarily objected to by or disruptive of any particular practice or way of life, is considered, on the scale of its aggregation, as irrational. A high-spirited party, spilling over onto the pathway in front of my house, is anti-social, not primarily because it disrupts my neighbours but because, taken as an action in reciprocal relation with its social aggregate, it is unacceptable; were such behaviour to be engaged in by everyone, there would not be sufficient path-space in front of the houses on the street to accommodate passersby. It detracts from Society by virtue of not being scalable.

The reciprocities of our time and place run vertically between individuals and Society, and not horizontally between beings in communities; as we download our survival strategies from social platforms, so we upload our calculated actions to the social cloud.

We speak now of finding friendship, or of finding love – not of finding a friend or a lover. In our relations with one another, we are mediated through the social possibility – friendship, love – which blocks horizontal interactions between beings with vertical strategies for realizing social abstractions. When I find friendship now, when I find love, the person with whom I find it has also found friendship, or found love. It is to friendship or to love that we appeal, which are generic possibilities, and not the friend or the lover, who are particular realities. This allows us – compels us, rather – to conduct the relation according to strategies of friendship, strategies of love, which, while ready-made and easy in one sense, do also bequeath to us a new and enervating task, a task that has come to be synonymous with the social, and which is fraught with the anxiety that is born of its impossibility: that of *connecting* my friendship with your friendship, my love with your love. Our devotion to connection is born of our rechannelling, as beings whose primary mode of relating is with Society, as social beings, such that the administrative satisfactions that we derive from together producing a friendship-effect or a love-effect are accompanied by a constant, low-level hum of dissatisfaction, at the poverty of our horizontal living, at the lack of meaningful interaction between us, at our sense that we have yet to find a friend.

We speak, in consequence, of real friendship, and of real love, but our yearning only leads us through another cycle of social strategizing. On Tinder, for example, men are more likely to attract positive attention if they include in their profile a photo of themselves, taken outdoors with a dog. Presumably, it makes them appear more 'real,' the descriptor which, if you recall, is the most commonly used in Tinder biographies. It is called 'dogfishing,' another strategy in the hopeless pursuit of real love. Such is the rigidity of our modes of interaction, they are effortlessly regulated by a limited stock of generic images and ideas offered to us on a plate by the social media to which we apply to solve the problems that it creates. The fact that inclusion of the descriptors 'spontaneous' and 'adventurous' also increase a man's chances of finding love on Tinder is just another of the ironies of our age. The greatest irony of which turns out to be that Society – the notional aggregate of ways of thinking and behaving, to which we contract out the rationality of our ways of thinking and behaving and which repays our misplaced trust with an endless stream of social solutions to social problems – Society is that which blocks interactions between beings.

The 'social,' for all that it names for us what is desirable in life, the 'play' that compensates for 'work,' that which brings us together, is that which first prised us and continues to prise us apart, that which mediates between us so that our interactions are rendered rigid and predictable rather than local and habitual, and requiring, therefore, of mediation. And much as we revel in our social skills, there is therefore always the underlying anxiety, that everything on which the meaning of our lives relies is something from which we might, at any moment, be locked out. We consult the wealth of guides, which promise us the *key* – to friendship, to love – because we sense that we are in play at the behest of Society and that Society can change the rules at any time, and that, if it does, we may find ourselves excluded, without any kind of friend, without even a friendship-effect. Not so many years ago, the language of 'reaching out' to one another began to enter our socially mediated interactions – 'I reached out to Jill the other day; hadn't seen her in a while.' Our language carries implicit acknowledgements, echoing sadly of our strangeness to one another. Reaching out, to what is not easily available, to what is retreating, to what may or may not be within our grasp. Social distancing seems a relatively new idea. But it ought not to. For, the social, despite its connotations to the contrary, is nothing other than distance.

*

And the child with autism feels it all: she who is defined by her failure to be social.

The child with autism is not, after all, incapable of reciprocity. Far from it. What she is incapable of is producing a reciprocity-effect, which requires social skills, that is, competence in the appropriate selection and application of social strategies. In a fulsomely supported way of life, in which such skilful recourse to social strategies would not be necessary, the young person with autism would be less likely to stand apart, unable to mingle with the crowd. What makes her stand apart from *us* – what makes her autistic, in other words – is the absence of meaningful support for our arrangements for living, which must be downloaded from generic social possibilities and experienced in relation to abstract social principles and constantly refreshed as those possibilities and principles are subject to sometimes drastic alteration.

Why can Joseph not answer that question about the book, when he can say the word 'book' and read the word 'book'? Why does he not respond? Why is it as if he has not even heard the question? Or as if, having heard it, it simply makes no sense? It is because the question, plucked from that context-less fund of content from which we select our social manoeuvres – the question, for Joseph, comes from nowhere. From out of the blue. Like all our social interactions, the question – asked by a visitor perhaps, in a well-meaning effort to engage – hangs in thin air. There is no being prepared for it. There is no run up to it. And there is, therefore, no answering it. There are only the strategies for dealing with it, surviving it. A winning smile, perhaps, like the children on TV; or a raucous shout, to attract further attention; or the word, 'Book,' in a tone that is cute or polite. Many strategies would do the job, but Joseph cannot strategize and so cannot produce an answer-effect to what is, after all, a question-effect.

Those of us who try to help children with autism to learn to respond to question-effects are taught to compensate for what question-effects lack; to simulate the props that they are so painfully without; to give them a context. Anything will help – the Makaton sign, the time of day, the tone of voice, the pregnant pause – anything, just to thicken the air of our so-called 'questions,' to anchor them, to prevent their appearing as if from outer space. Indeed, our care of children with autism is dominated by efforts of this kind, inventing and adhering to routines, adding substance to the anaemic quality of our daily lives in which so much is dispensable and subject to alteration or suspension. The professionals call this enterprise 'scaffolding,' a metaphor derived satisfyingly from the physical world, the very world that we have retreated from so hastily, and so disastrously. But, though it certainly helps to pursue this enterprise with energy and determination, it is bedevilled by its inherently contradictory aim: that of producing a way-of-life-effect.

The scaffolding that those of us who care for children with autism so carefully construct around them will always fall short of the way of life whose absence it would compensate for. It is too flimsy; we sometimes renege upon its promises as you can never renege upon the sun or the soil or the festival. Or it is too rigid, a prison, to which we cleave as we never would when the sun sets or the soil is frozen solid or the festival comes to a close. Our way of life effects are not organic; they are not natural. They are not bound to people and places and times and things at a myriad points. Too often they are upright when they should bend, and too often they bend when they should resist. No artificial construct can replicate the rise and fall of people who really live together in a real world.

So the child with autism is unpersuaded, even by the most carefully crafted of our scaffolding strategies – she cannot cope, she has meltdowns. These are distressing, of course. But buried in their disfunction is a sustained and inspiring instinctual project: that of stripping away the strategies, of fighting them off, to get to some experience of reciprocity lying beneath.

How can you tell a young person with autism from a distance? Likely he is walking on his toes, with that forward sloping gait, so characteristic, with that unblunted capacity to feel and to negotiate pressure. It explains his penchant for tiny spaces; for being wedged in. And it is the reason he jumps. For joy: in the great kickback of the earth; in the elemental reciprocity of pressure exerted and returned; in the spring, the support, of the ground beneath our feet. Joseph jumps up and down and wrings, as we no longer do, a kind of life blood from the stone itself. To allay the terrible transience all around. To offset the infinite flexibility of our rigidly strategic Society.

6

Self

Around the middle of the seventeenth century, on a winter's day in Amsterdam, a man sat lost in thought. His stove was lit, the sparks from its fuel nudging at the silence. A pot of coffee waited on top, infusing the room. The man wore his dressing gown, its wool bristling his wrists. His feet rested gingerly on the fender, just at that delicious temperature that is not quite too hot for touch. All his senses, soothed. His whole body, seen to.

Then, in defiance of it all – of his senses so gently in play, of his body so carefully tended – the man who was lost in thought supposed that none of it was real. Not the stove with its crackling heat. Not the coffee - not its taste, not its smell. Not the abrasions of his gown, nor the near-painful pleasure of his toasting toes. The man who was lost in thought supposed it all might be a dream. That his body and its senses might only deceive.

For this man who was lost in thought, only one thing was really real: thought. The stove might not be hot and might not be a stove. But his thought that there is a stove and it is hot must be the thought that there is a stove and it is hot. The stove might not exist. But the thought about the stove cannot not exist. Not only that, while this man who was lost in thought was having the thought about the stove and its being hot, he too must have existed.

I am thinking, therefore I am.

Thus it was that on a cold day in Amsterdam all but four hundred years ago there rose from the ashes of a stove's fire and the dregs of a pot's coffee and the threads of a wool gown and the last rusting fragments of a fender – from the imagined demolition of a scene of sensory consolation – that which was destined to be the realest thing of all, though it could not be touched or tasted or heard or smelt or seen: 'I.'

What was this 'I' that seemed to have proven itself so real? It was not the body in the dressing gown, its tongue laced with coffee and its toes pink with cheer. The body and its tongue and its toes were all of them cast in doubt. They may have been hallucinations. Delirium. The senses tell us lies. No - the 'I' that was thinking that its tongue tastes and its toes toast had nothing to do with the body and tongues and toes. It was something far more ghostly, for all that it was judged also far more real. It was the mind.

The mind has been a fugitive since the days of Descartes. For one thing, the biological sciences have meanwhile begun to open up the bodies of dead people – and of live people – to see and to fix what is going on inside. Once that was done, more and more of the ghostly mind was brought down to earth, tied to synapses and neurons and the like. Bits of body. We have chased the mind to its hiding places. But the mind has not been caught. It has, in fact, retreated further into the mists, shuffling off its outer garments when we have presumed to have grounded it, and remaining in essence the same incorporeal repository of all things real and true – I, my *self*.

Today, if I have sex with someone of the opposite sex, *I am* heterosexual. If I talk at parties, *I am* extrovert. If I avoid crowded scenes, *I am* phobic. And if I do not interact strategically, *I am* autistic. All these *I am*s, which add nothing of content to what might just as easily roam as discrete behaviours, contingent habits – sex with men, talking at parties, keeping to open spaces, avoiding small talk – but which plug those habits into a mysterious entity – I, my *self* – which elevates them to the status of holy truth and makes them more than a little awkward to dislodge. To suddenly have sex with a woman becomes a big deal, something to be talked about, worked through, understood.

*

And so we come to the other of our polar institutions, opposite to the institution of Society and its great compliment. If Society is that which circulates the concepts, labels and signals of our pillar institutions, providing the strategies to download them and to put them into play, the Self is the place in which those abstractions are lodged and come to rest, coating their generality in a homely hue, balancing the grandeur of their *social* significance with the intimacy of their *personal* truth. Together, Society and Self constitute the vertical axis that scrambles our horizontal meanings so that human interaction is the interaction of Selves as mediated by the Society with which they are in primary relation.

And the great irony is that the young person diagnosed with autism – whose situation is named after the Greek word for 'self' and whose behaviours so often manifest as selfish – is defined most of all by her exclusion from this institution, by her not having a Self, by her being gloriously free of this secular soul in which the rest of us implicitly believe.

*

Thirty years ago, the Cambridge neuroscientist Simon Baron-Cohen produced an account of what it is like to be autistic. It summarized the condition by claiming that young people with autism do not have a 'theory of mind.' A simple experiment was used to illustrate the point. In it, a group of four-year-olds was confronted with a scene in which there were two dolls, each with a basket. The first doll placed a marble in its basket and left the scene. The second doll, while the first doll was absent, took the marble out of the first doll's basket and put it into its basket. The first doll returned. The question was, where would the first doll go to retrieve the marble. The non-autistic four-year-olds answered that the first doll would go to its basket for the marble. The autistic four-year-olds answered that the first doll would go to the second doll's basket for the marble.

The non-autistic four-year-olds in Baron-Cohen's experiment seemed to interpret the returning first doll by attributing to her certain states of mind; aware that the first doll could not know that the marble had been moved, they judged her to expect the marble to still be in her basket and be confused when she found that it was not. The autistic four-year-olds did not appear to attribute to the returning doll any mental states; what the doll might know, what it might expect, did not seem to strike them. The information that they used to anticipate the doll's retrieval of the marble seemed therefore wholly dominated by where the marble actually was. The marble was now in the second doll's basket and so it was to the second doll's basket that the first doll would go to retrieve it.

What this seemed to show is that young people with autism are unable to 'see' the minds of other people, that young people with autism are, as Baron-Cohen expressed it, 'mind blind.'

I think that this is right. Admittedly, autism occurs on the infamous 'spectrum,' so it may be more or less right as a description of those with the diagnosis. In the main, however, it seems accurate to say that young people with autism do not have a 'theory of mind.'

The question is, whether this is to be regretted. Whether this is a disability. Or whether we might consider that it is having a 'theory of mind' that is regrettable and disabling.

What is it, after all, to 'see minds'? It is to interpret and interact with other people on the basis of the attribution to them of states of mind that are presumed to shape their involvement in the cut and thrust of life, states of mind that are somehow prior to or removed from the cut and thrust of life, that give form to life in abstract ways. If we are able to 'see minds,' therefore, other people are for us primarily theoretical beings; in relating to them, it is the presumed abstract framework of their experiences that is our heuristic.

Might we pause to consider the potential poverty of this mode of relating to other people? Its propensity for rigidity and for the blockage of meaningful interaction? What must we bypass, what must we dull down, in order to achieve it? And are those diagnosed as autistic – those who are 'mind blind' – in fact the incubators of modes of interaction that are fulsome, immediate and lived when compared with our theoretical relations?

But the stakes are higher here even than we might suppose. After all, the first person to see minds did not see other minds. He saw his own. To have a theory of mind is first and foremost to have a theory of your own mind.

We might think that we do not need a theory of our own mind, that our own mind is simply there for us – immediately, directly. And yet, how difficult it was for Descartes, to see his own mind. How much he had to relinquish just to do so; how abstract and implausible,

150

how theoretical, his suppositions had to be. The whole of his body's experience, everything his senses provided – the warmth, the comfort, the sight and the smell of the world – reneged upon, bracketed off, cast in doubt. Just so he could see his own mind.

Who would do this? Who would take this trouble? Who would sacrifice the consolations of sensory existence for the sake of seeing their mind? Very few indeed, Descartes presumed; it was to be a rarified experiment. He wrote an account of his stoveside musings in Latin, not his native French, which is the language that he otherwise used for writing. Descartes anticipated that his fireside meditations would be of interest only to a few, to those removed from the cut and thrust of life, those privileged enough to have received a Classical education and at ease enough to employ it. Only they might be extracted from the world's fray sufficiently to amputate their body, to enter that meditative state in which sensory experience can be dialled back to zero, to be persuaded that a theoretical construct is more real than anything that can be touched and tasted and heard and smelt and seen.

If you have spent your day laying stone blocks on top of one another so that your palms are hardened by callouses, or kneading bread to the correct elasticity, you will be unlikely to leap into the experiment that none of that is real. Only the leisured classes, those already half-removed from the touch and feel of life, would bother with the effort of seeing their mind. Only those already disenchanted with the world...

For, what was it, after all, that Descartes managed to 'see' upon sacrificing the world as given by his senses? Only thoughts. Nothing more than thoughts. The sparks of a fire, but without their enlivening crackle; the rub of a gown, but without its bracing abrasion; the smell of coffee, but without its bittersweet promise; the temperature of toes, but without its optimal tingle. What Descartes 'saw' were only abstractions, treachery against literal seeing: theoretical sparks, theoretical abrasions, theoretical smells, theoretical heat. All that was left of bodied existence once his body was taken out of play. Ghosts of bodied experience; spectres of the material world; shells of sensory life.

Mere scraps, then; leftovers: that is what Descartes saw when he took the trouble of seeing his mind. Abstract forms emptied of life, a hangover from the obliteration of the world by the diminishment of the body. What Descartes named as the realest thing of all – thinking and the mind that is its home – was, therefore, nothing at all in its own right. It owed its existence entirely to the suspension of the experiences of his body, for it comprised nothing but the abstract traces of those experiences. Descartes could see his mind only by switching off his body because Descartes had a mind only by switching off his body so that its empty forms remained. The mind whose existence Descartes said cannot be in doubt was a wholly artificial entity, called forth by a great feat of abstraction from all things corporeal, born of the body that had to die to give it life.

Descartes' mind was never anything other than a theoretical construct. A theory. To see your own mind was, from the very start, to have a theory of your own mind. There was never anything easier or more immediate about seeing your own mind than there was about seeing the minds of others. For, the mind was a theoretical phenomenon. There was no mind until there was a theory of mind.

*

None of this may resonate with us, this great effort to see the mind, to be entered into only by a few. For us, it is everyday fare. For us, it really does come naturally – immediately, directly.

But perhaps we ought to ask why this is so? Are we so disenchanted with the world that its sacrifice no longer feels like one?

Who toasts their toes any more? Whose wrists are rubbed by the rough grain of a wool gown? Whose coffee brews in their garret room? Who sits without endless distraction by virtual possibilities? Who lays block on block until their palms crust over? Who kneads their daily bread? Are we not already initiated into the dial-back of bodied experience that Descartes had to work so hard to cast in doubt? Are our lives not more or less abstract lives already. For us the mind is a natural phenomenon because the disabling of the body that is the price of its existence has been woven into our world and our style of living in it.

Bodies do intrude, of course, even now, even in their wholesale suspension at the altar of the mind. But they intrude only as refracted through minds, only, therefore, as theoretical bodies; like the sparks of Descartes' fire and the rub of Descartes' gown, bodies are experienced only in theory, their manifestations, their secretions, their movements, experienced as the secondary characteristics, the mere symptoms, of states of mind – tiredness, as the result of thinking sad thoughts; and beating hearts, as the effect of thinking that there is danger. As if toasting toes are the result of thinking that it is hot.

What an irony there is at the centre of our great talent for seeing minds. States of body are emptied out, rendered theoretical as states of mind, which then, in their turn, render states of body as their slaves, as the mere signs or symptoms of the states of mind that were constituted by abstracting from them. A self-perpetuating cycle of disembodiment thus ensues, in which states of body are gradually eroded in their richness by being continually interpreted as outputs of abstract versions of themselves.

As we have grown accustomed to ignoring the call of our body, the call of our body has grown every day less insistent, more generic, more abstract, made almost insensible by the smooth, ergonomic, touch-sensitive, user-friendly character of our frictionless world. This, in the end, has the effect of making our body states abstract, to reflect our states of mind, though, in the beginning, it was states of mind that were abstract versions of states of body.

This spiral of abstraction, the gradual disembodiment of our experiences, explains why we have so forgotten the artificiality of minds as to find it natural to see them. Over four hundred years of reducing our bodies to the mere representatives of their theoretical manifestations, gradually diluting the richness of bodied existence so that it approaches in its materiality the immateriality of its mental equivalents, we have been formed – deformed – to see minds.

Perhaps now we may begin to realize why this great ability of ours, to see minds, might not, after all, be just an ability. Its price is a great and global disability. To call forth the mind, you must disable your body. To see minds, you must not see bodies. You must pull back from the richness of the world as given to you by your senses and be satisfied instead by dried out shells of lived experience.

To see minds requires a life of remove from the material world, from the things that kick back at you, from the nut that will not fit its bolt, from the needle that pierces your finger, from the fire that sparks and burns, from those experiences that animate your body and are animated by your body in their turn. The cycle of animation of body and world must be dulled. The things that meet you half-way, the supports that prop you up helpfully but insistently, must be pushed aside, their demands so muted that they come to seem unreal. It is why our fire now blazes on a flat-screen TV.

We should after all regret the comfort of Descartes' body as he sat by his stove and savoured his coffee. He was too comfortable. Too well seen to. Too at ease. The world was too lenient. The body too leisurely. If the abrasions of his gown had only been harsher, the heat of his stove more intense, his coffee more bitter. As it was, he was halfway to that curious disability, that dullness of the senses, which for us, now, is second nature. Here was a man for whom nothing that could be touched or tasted or smelt or heard or seen was in that moment available to him with the intensity that leaves no room for doubt, that carries us away.

Poor Descartes, with his body tuned down. Poor Descartes, for whom the scratch of winter wool was infinitely more real without its scratch. Poor Descartes – body blind.

And poor us, Descartes' inheritors, who live within his great experiment, who live and die lost in thought. Our bodies already suspended. So at ease in their elasticated clothing and their sink-into sofas and their snacking and grazing and the thermostat that never burns hot or cold.

Poor us, with tongues blunted by food that looks and tastes like the cartons it comes in. And sinuses burned by air fresheners and perfumes, and ears drowned out by advertisements and admonishments. Poor us, our bodies killed by the drop-down, ready-made, click-through kindnesses of institutional provenance, for whom the realest version of everything is its theoretical possibility, its abstract distillation, its mental state.

*

What is it that can have animated these dry theoretical possibilities, so otherwise devoid of life? From where do they derive their energy that, dessicated as they are, they have overcome the rich plenty that might be given through our body's senses? What has made us resist the smell of freshly ground and brewed coffee, resting on the stovetop to keep its heat, so as to reach for its cardboard equivalent? What has made us turn from the fulsomeness of a world experienced through our bodies, to favour instead its abstract counterpart, not fulsome, not rich, not a feast for the senses at all?

The answer lies in that very repository that Descartes saw as implied by his thinking: I, my *self*, the site from which our theoretical relations with ourselves, others and the world derive their originary force, the unifying principle that gives to our experiences an irresistible atmosphere of unassailable truth, and a power over us that belies their dry and generic character. I am thinking, therefore I am – so Descartes concluded. And ever since, the pull of thinking is explained by its alleged guarantee, that I am. We have put the cart before the horse, in other words, and remain within Descartes' thought experiment for the mysterious self-center with which it is infused. I am, therefore I submit to thinking – tantalized by the promise of the self, we have accepted abstraction as its cost. We have sacrificed our body as the price of our self, and relinquished the rich abundance of sensory life for the assurance that each of us is *I*.

Yet the price that we pay is never quite enough. Not to dispel the lingering fear, that Descartes got it wrong, that he went a step too far, that his certainty that I am thinking never really did imply that I am; that even if he was justified in seeing thinking, once he had suspended all feeling, that even then he was not justified in seeing the mind, the thing that does the thinking, that has the thinking, that causes the thinking – me, my self, I. Descartes' radical doubt experiment, which set at naught his material being, may not have got in return the immaterial self that we have all been so taken by. After all that effort, after dulling our bodies to see its dry and abstract traces, there may never have been anything else to see at all; the mind, *I*, an improbable mirage.

Is this why our blind faith in the existence of *I* – my self – has been dogged by a constant worry, by a niggling sense that it is, somehow, always out of reach? Is it why our dazzlement with the promise of *I* is ever infused with a troubled sense of its unreality? Is it why we are constantly urged to *find* our self, and to *believe* in our self, and why we have got more and more lost in thought, burrowing deeper and more cravenly into the abstractions that are to be the guarantee: that I exist, that I am?

Unable by now to contemplate life without our modern soul, unable to countenance that there might, in the end, be no real me, we have accepted with greater enthusiasm every day the emptying out of the material world, of sensory existence, and its replacement by theoretical possibilities, virtual equivalents. We have acquiesced in the derealization of our world as the price of the realization of our self. The more abstract our previously bodied experiences have become – the more picture-perfect our frozen meal, the more Instagram-ready our children, our dog, our house, our face – the more our lives have been lost to abstraction, lost in thought, the more assured we feel that we *are,* that there is an *I,* deep down inside, the reference point for these abstract experiences, at once their container and their compensation. We have accepted the emptying out of our world for its implied promise that we really do exist.

*

The worry endures, though. Descartes went too far and that cannot be patched over for long. But the worry is as effective as the measures that we take to assuage it, consigning us, who live in the slipstream of Descartes' meditations, to that flip-flop of fragility and resilience that is what we call 'identity,' the very endgame of the self. We gradually come to place our experiences within the context of our 'identity,' which makes us a curious combination of vulnerable and unyielding, susceptible and stalwart. We are injured at every slight, hardly able to stand the briefest encounter with a hard surface, made for floating, unimpeded, in the frosty ether of internet virtue, where only the gentlest, emptiest, most abstract, possibilities prevail – 'man' and 'woman' now too specific to be tolerated, aggressions against our identity. Yet we are steeled at every turn for greater fortitude, as drastic changes in trends of working, socializing, understanding and articulating cut so deep into who we are that we must invent ourselves all over again from the inside out – experience ourselves as gender-dysphoric when we had previously not been interested in boys; experience ourselves as autistic when we had heretofore passed off as shy – and to welcome our reinvention as a liberation, as an unearthing of the true me.

One of the companies that provides buses in my city is running an advertising campaign entitled #*buspeople*. It is not really for promoting bus travel; the buses, now often empty, are billboards, advertising something else. Promoting a new kind of being, or doubling down on the promotion of what is, by now, an old kind of being. Selling us our *self*. *She is The Multi-Tasker,* the campaign goes. *He is The Last-Minuter. Which one are you?* And then a link to the site where you can complete a questionnaire, to discover who you really are. The real you, to be determined by a ten-question form languishing on the website of a failing regional bus company – hardly in human history has the nature of the human been so defiled. And all under the aegis of its supposed promotion, protection, recognition, liberation.

How thoughtless the bus company's designators are. How uninventive, how un-special – The Multi-Tasker, The Last-Minuter. Yet the designators of the life sciences and management sciences to which we apply to know our identity are hardly more edified. The Phobic, The Bisexual, The Team-Player, The Autistic. All these identifiers, sold to us crassly as keys to our mystical selves, trite descriptions of the modern soul. Degrading in themselves, but also – worst of all – utterly vulnerable to interference. As we are enjoined to *help our self*, *improve our self*, even to *update our self*, our self, for the sake of which we have sacrificed our world, is revealed as a mere port for the most recent generic themes of our institutions.

The gentle promise of the mind – its delicate vulnerability – is allied with a hard-nosed worldly pragmatism; its atmosphere of unassailable truth curiously twinned with susceptibility to constant revision. Pegging us inexorably to the concepts, signals and labels of sexuality, gender, intelligence, orientation, race – themes increasingly delivered to us by the biological sciences and the businesses that feed off them, at whose alter all other institutions, even the institutions of education, now kneel. So that – greatest irony of all – we who more than any other humans in history, believe in our own uniqueness – there's only one you – are more than any other humans in history generic, predictable, alike – defined by the abstractions of the management and life sciences. Bio-beings, business-beings, indexed to a mysterious core that only these sciences can articulate and understand. We can see minds, yes, but the minds are theoretical constructs and the theories that allow us to see them are bio-theories and business theories whose provenance and plausibility we are woefully ill-equipped to recognise or judge.

And we must move with the latest research, of course, in the bio-sciences and the business sciences – adapt to conform with their latest findings. The most artificial, most careless inventions of an MBA student at a prestigious university must be downloaded into your self, as your self. The latest experimental product must be injected into your self, as your self. In cleaving to who we really are, we open ourselves to being constantly reformatted, sites for the implantation of the most up-to-date research whether in libraries or laboratories or both.

And all of this tinkering, to which we are endlessly subject, is haunted by the chilling spectre of our being erased, wiped out, no longer visible or audible, shadow-banned, cancelled. Our Self can be cancelled – I, who *am* with all of the certainty that Descartes could muster, can be cancelled. The hotch-potch of identifications of which we are comprised, deemed false. It turns out that our experience of salvation at being plugged in to another category or another pill – finally, I feel myself; at last, I know who I am – draws its hyperbole from that underlying dread that there will come a day when we find ourselves plugged out.

In the meantime, as we frantically remake ourselves to avoid our obliteration, our experiences retreat further from us, further beyond our grasp; what it is like to be me, more and more alien to me. We are urged to 'own' our experiences but owning them is by way of framing them with the latest scientistic categories, the latest theory of mind. By owning our experiences, we make them available for tweaking and transformation. Our unhappiness, as a state of our mind, becomes a theoretical phenomenon – I am a depressive – crying and tiredness reduced to the uncertain, merely contingent status of symptoms. Our anxiety, as a state of our mind, becomes an abstract expression of someone who is a neurotic – palpitations and shortness of breath consigned to its might-be-there-or-not bodily manifestations. Even our joy becomes an abstract possibility – I'm hyper; I'm caffeine-sensitive. We understand our experiences by attributing them to mental states, and by unifying those states in a single identity; by so doing, we are removed from the bodily intimacy of our experiences, which is consigned to a secondary status, a derivation.

BE YOURSELF – more than any other, this injunction captures what freedom is in our time. It appears to express a tautology. How could we be anything else? But it is in fact an oxymoron. We are destined to the doubling that Descartes set in train for us, destined never to be our self; for, our self is premised upon the suppression of all that might contribute to our being, to experience as given by our senses, in favour of the false promises held out by products of institutional research. BE YOUSELF – the great lie of our uniqueness, of that psychological barcode which guarantees who we really are, of our identity.

What is our 'identity' really? It is the promise of uniqueness – but only insofar as it is the crossing point of a finite number of utterly generic, theoretically established characteristics. I am Introvert, Bisexual, Sensitive, Middle-Born, Left-Brain, Blood-Type A+, etc. etc. At the notional intersection of these generic renderings of personal orientations and talents lies my uniqueness, my identity, me. But the notional intersection is precisely that: notional, theoretical, abstract. Which means that the experience of myself and others as identities renders me and others into notional, theoretical, abstract beings, conduits for the most generic behaviours and attitudes under the vague certainty that their configuration as they pass through me constitutes a one-off real me.

I am thinking, therefore I am: so famous an insight that even its Latin rendition – *Cogito ergo sum* – is familiar to us all.

But there is something unsettling in this familiarity, in the all-pervasiveness of what is one of the most counter-intuitive, radically abstract, rarefied insights in Western philosophy. Who could have known that it would be taken up so widely? Who would have predicted that it would have carried the day?

I shall think, Descartes proposed, *that the sky, the air, the earth, colours, shapes, sounds and all external things are merely delusions which he has devised to ensnare my judgment. I shall consider myself as not having hands or eyes, or flesh, or blood or senses, but as falsely believing that I have all these things.*

What an irony, that the experiment of doubting all external things, all things of the material world as provided to us by our body's senses, that this experiment of doubting all things as if they were delusions visited upon us by a conspirator against us has rendered us wholly vulnerable to the delusions visited upon by those who conspire against us – that our willingness to set the world at naught, to second-guess the certainties of our body, has made us so susceptible to the ensnarement of our judgment, the manipulation of and by the mind that is our Self.

Like the autistic that we are, our eyes glaze over at the sight of the world – we will not attend to it, it will not get through to us, it is blocked out – and alight instead on the most abstract of possibilities, whose rigidity we mistake for reality and whose endless exchangeability we mistake for life.

*

Can we retrace our steps? Undo the harm that has been done? Four centuries is quite a span. Too long, probably, to awaken Descartes from his fateful meditations and unravel the legacy of his unlikely experiment. But thirty years is not too long. At least we might undo the legacy of Baron-Cohen's experiment.

There was something obviously wrong about Baron-Cohen's experiment. Something that was right before our eyes, which yet we did not notice. Right in the middle of the room. It was the dolls. The *dolls*. Inanimate pseudo-humans, crafted along the most generic lines, with faces like the face of everyone, bodies smooth and lifeless. The non-autistic four-year-olds attributed to these dolls a range of mental states; they 'saw' the dolls' minds. But dolls do not have mental states. Dolls do not have minds.

The non-autistic four-year-olds all made the same mistake. By misattributing to the dolls certain expectations and confusions, they did not distinguish between beings that can expect things and those that cannot. A doll cannot expect anything. The autistic four-year-olds at least did not make this mistake. They did not interpret dolls as beings that might anticipate something. The autistic four-year-olds got it right about the dolls.

How could the non-autistic four-year-olds be so ready to see minds as to see them even in dolls, in smoothed out, lifeless things? What might explain what was in fact their failure in Baron-Cohen's experiment? Is the dubious ability to 'see minds,' which is what the experiment establishes autistic people as unable to do, is this dubious ability in fact indifferent to life, riding roughshod over bodies as the mere formal occasion for the projection of abstract possibilities? Was the non-autistic four-year-olds' readiness to experience the dolls as having minds the effect of their successful initiation – at such a young age – into the experience of *selves*, chimerical collections of theoretical possibilities independent of living flesh and blood?

We might object that the non-autistic four-year-olds saw the dolls' minds, unconcerned by their dead, makeshift bodies, because the non-autistic four-year-olds 'saw' that that is what the humans conducting the experiment expected them to see. In other words, the non-autistic four-year-olds' readiness to identify the dolls' mental states was derived from, and repeated, the non-autistic four-year-olds' readiness to identify the scientists' mental states.

But what does this make of Baron-Cohen's experiment? Was it not more akin to a kind of initiation ceremony, an exercise in the derealization upon which the ability to see minds is premised, in which success – the correct answer – was determined by the extent to which living humans and dead dolls can be interpreted, alike, as having minds, the ingredient of living, breathing flesh and blood taken out of play? A propaganda exercise, then, as may be all our role play and tea party fun, which inure young children to the habit of seeing minds where there are none, so that those who are not disabled in this respect learn to experience themselves and each other as living dolls, whose animation principle is the soul that lies within and that owes its existence entirely to the theory that we have of it.

Meanwhile, the autistic four-year-olds did not see any minds in Baron-Cohen's experiment. They did not see the minds of the dolls and were utterly unmoved by the dolls in any way. Probably, they did not see the dolls as stand-ins for humans. After all, dolls' supposed similarity to humans is premised upon our practiced substitution of dolls for humans in our initiation ceremonies of the seeing of minds – in which ceremonies children with autism usually cannot participate at all. And the autistic four-year-olds did not see the minds of the humans, the scientists conducting the experiment, because, for autistic young people, human beings do not have minds. They have bodies.

Indeed, given the intensely bodied character of autistic experience, how on earth were the autistic four-year-olds even able to simulate participation in Baron-Cohen's experiment? Were they sitting still? Often, they do not, unless they are held down. Were they looking at the scene unfolding before them, or were they staring at the fluorescent ceiling light, or the recording camera, or the watch on the wrist of the experimenter? Were they listening to the scientists' instructions, or to the hum of the boiler? Were they absorbed in readjusting the waistband of their jeans? Autistic four-year-olds' bodies cannot simply be switched off. Their sensory experience – overload, we call it – is such that they cannot easily be deadened to enable attention to be paid to the abstract scenarios that we are now so continuously expected to orient ourselves towards, and from the earliest age. How much were the autistic four-year-olds really engaged in Baron-Cohen's experiment? It was, after all, as dramatic and implausible a scenario for dialling back bodied existence in favour of theoretical possibilities as was Descartes' thought experiment, in which even he presumed that none but a few privileged and curious might be able to be involved.

And then there was all of the language used in the experiment: *Sit children. Now, in a moment, we will ask you to watch a little play...* Did the autistic four-year-olds follow this language? Did they even notice that they were being addressed? Might it not as well have been in Latin, for all they knew of it? At six, Joseph would have no ability to comprehend a set of spoken instructions. Nor does he give signs of doing so. Who *were* the autistic four-year-olds in Baron-Cohen's experiment?

Even supposing that they were able to hear the scientists' instructions, and to understanding the question about where the first doll would go to look for the marble –

and this supposition is an unlikely one – even supposing this, their overwhelming impulse would have been to make the instructions and the questions go away, to make the language stop. *Marble – Basket*, they would have heard, and in desperation they would have pointed at the basket with the marble in it.

It would have been a mighty effort – even that – to play a game that was designed to exclude them. For, Baron-Cohen's was a self-fulfilling experiment, claiming to establish what it already presumed, directing a scenario reliant upon the dominance of the spoken word and the dialling back of the body and then using it to establish that some children (those who do not connect with the spoken word and whose bodies are not dialled back) are unable to answer correctly the question the experiment aimed to ask.

If this self-fulfilling experiment were a rarefied one, bounded by the parameters of abstract scientific research, that would be one thing. The tragedy is that its dolls' world is, in many ways, an accurate microcosm of our world, to negotiate which requires the kind of expertise in the refraction of body-states through their mental-state equivalents that, for us, now counts as normal experience. Sitting before Baron-Cohen's tableau, the autistic four-year-olds, to the extent that they were autistic, were undoubtedly tuned out, turned off, disengaged. Their eyes were vacant if they were not alight with sensory input entirely irrelevant to the scene; their ears were muffled if they were not pricked by some sound out of doors or in the plumbing. They were autistic in respect of Baron-Cohen's experiment – in respect of its basic premises and not only of its specific targets. And they are autistic in respect of the world generally – their eyes glaze over, their ears tune out, their touch is blunted, their taste dulled and their smell deadened – unless some marginal eventuality, sudden light or note or rough or sweet or spice, brings them to life. Because this autistic coming to life is not the one that we expect – it is not the one that our society sets us up for – we judge it to be the effect of sensory overload, of confusion, of disability, and we train the eyes and ears of our children with autism all the more eagerly towards the theoretical abstractions, the lifeless interactions, the generic possibilities, that count for us as life, but that are as dead as the dolls and as unabsorbing.

We expend so much of our energy in drawing in these children who will not attend, to what is, in effect, the longest and most drawn out thought experiment in history. How long more, before their persistent lack of interest in it makes us question whether it is, in fact, worthy of interest, and whether we who are now so adept at performing our interest in it have been severed from the sensory life that those children diagnosed as autistic continue to incubate and to demonstrate on our behalf?

I will imagine it is all a delusion, Descartes wrote. And so it became a delusion, our predictable, generic world in which the body plays so little part, in which there really is little point in taking notice. We should attend to our children who see this, who see that the rest of us are so often like dolls, our involvements about as interesting as the project of the marble and the baskets, mechanically enacting plans and projects of inhuman dimensions, rigid in our movements, blocked in our interactions.

And we should probably stop calling *them* autistic.

*

There is no way on earth to teach Joseph about states of mind. That I might be angry if he does this or that, is not for him. That he might be distressed because of a disappointed expectation does not, as we say, compute. These abstract mappings, of experiences rendered as mental states onto events or objects in the world, do not speak to him.

When Joseph is joyful – watching the water drain from the bath or the Nicholas Brothers go through their tap routine – he jumps for joy. Fast, like a boxer skipping in training. The reverberations that are sent through the soles of his feet and up through his body – grounding the excitement and increasing it – are his joy. He does not smile and say that he likes it. He does not reflect on it. He is not outside of his joy. He is in it. He is it. It is the same with anger, which, for Joseph, is clenched fists and gritted teeth. A state of body, not of mind.

According to Baron Cohen, children with autism are incapable of what he terms 'cognitive empathy' – empathy of the mind, in other words. Such children achieve only what Baron Cohen describes as 'affective empathy' – empathy of the body. But what, after all, is cognitive empathy, of which autistic children are incapable? Is it empathy really? Or is it, in fact, a substitute for empathy, a theoretical framing of another's suffering such that it cannot get at me at all? I am thinking, therefore I cannot feel. Children with autism are often presumed to be uncaring, unsympathetic. But, though it is true that Joseph cannot *see* that someone is sad if, by seeing it, we mean having a theory of the person's state of mind, he does sometimes cry when he is sorry for someone crying. He is with them in the feeling, though the markers that we use to determine whether he 'cognizes' it are absent.

Even we laugh sometimes when others laugh – not because we understand what they are laughing about, but because their laughter is infectious – it captures our body without being admitted by our minds. And sometimes we cry when others cry. Not often. And sometimes we grimace when a toddler gets an injection. Otherwise, how immune we are to others – to their experiences of despair or pain or happiness. How unmoved by it. How distant. How blocked from entering into it – really sharing in it – by our theoretical understandings. Our ability to see minds is a rather autistic ability, is it not, which blocks our interactions with others and makes our responses to them rigid, predictable and coldly bound by abstraction. Meanwhile, those who receive a diagnosis of 'autism' – are they not insufficiently autistic, demonstrating all that we have almost lost, capable of feeling with us, of being with us in our experiences of one another and the world, of being affected?

Perhaps the endgame of our disembodiment in the service of the mind has come in the caricature of bodies as convenient summaries of mental states – in all those 'emojis' which relieve us of even the small effort of articulating our cognitive empathy with ourselves and others by offering us a drop-down list of the simplest of body drawings. How rigid our interactions that apply to this list. How impeded and poor. And what an assault upon the depth and range of our states of body, that they are rendered so cartoonishly and placed in the service of our theories of mind.

We do not feel this outrage, we whose states of body are no longer rich and varied. We do not feel the degradation of the emoji. For, we have no sense of the body's potential. Of the range of experiences of which it is capable. We are stiff of body, and limited. More like those dolls, really, whose limbs move in straitened ways, and whose rigid frame is so unyielding to our various plans for them. As if we are entombed, our bodies – so young – consigned to a half-life at best, in which the full gamut of orientations and movements is not available. As if our joints need oiling.

Michel Serres reports on conversations that he had with people that he met during his travels, who asked with innocent curiosity whether we Westerns are taught in school to move in the way that we do – the natural circularity of our bodies' motions narrowed down and straightened out so that only a few stilted possibilities remain. As if we are, from an early age, preparing for the narrow grave; as if rigor mortis gradually encroaches.

But still we dismiss the lessons enacted by those children who we label 'autistic.' Still, we judge the extraordinary capabilities of their bodies as unwieldy, clumsy. The relative entombment of our bodies has been normalised. In a Society of Selves, the body seems always ill-disciplined.

Body states are quite alien to us now, outside of the moments of hyperbolic performance given to us by social strategies – the clap, quite worn out; the cheer, though even that has in recent years been superseded by movements borrowed from computer games or celebrity sports stars. Still, there is documentary evidence that it was not always thus. Our fairy tales are full of body states. Rumplestilskin stamps his foot through the floor when his plan is foiled; the little pigs roll around with high spirits; Thumbelina holds her head in her hands and weeps. Our traditional tales describe states of body that read for us with our disdain for the body, for us who only speak our minds, like cliché, pantomime, ham acting, implausibly overdone. Nobody does that, we think.

This harshness in our judgment of body states leads us to the common impression of children with autism as clumsy. They do not walk straight or sit still. It is all gambolling about, leaning this way and then that. Feet, not drawn by gravity to the floor, but tucked under thighs or swung up in the air or otherwise brought into play as ours so rarely are. When out walking, our projects are not salient to children with autism: the need to get somewhere in time, or to follow the gravelled path. They are brought to a halt by a flickering street light, or they crane their head round at the sound of music, or they wander onto the grass after a pattern in its tufts that we do not notice at all. Yes, children with autism do seem very clumsy.

Yet, there are times when Joseph's comportment is astounding. Aged three, he would recreate yoga movements that he had seen me go through in my room, although he had never appeared to be watching me closely. By age four – though he certainly could not have begun to participate in Baron Cohen's experiment – he could recreate my half-hour routine almost to perfection, with the smallest of details attended to. And he moves among the chairs under the kitchen table, with the flexibility of a being for whom standing on two legs is not the default, never upsetting anything, and seeming, on his travels, to get to know this domestic environment to its every contour. As one might if one were blind and making the necessary preparations to live there. Well,

Joseph is mind-blind, and therefore gloriously free to feel the world with his body.

The children who we label with autism do not suffer from sensory overload. It is we who suffer, from sensory underload. The children who we label with autism do not suffer from attention-deficit. It is we who suffer, from too much attention to what is not real. The children who we label with autism do not suffer from mind-blindness. It is we who suffer, from body-blindness. For the children who we label with autism, the rub of wool against their wrists and the sting of hot iron against their toes have a truth, a reality, an interest, that is not to be disregarded; what they feel with their bodies is intense and fulsome and – most vital of all – utterly beyond doubt. For the children who we label with autism, gifted as they are, it is not all a delusion.

7

Ending

In Dickens' *Our Mutual Friend*, there is a character called Sloppy. Indeed, if the novel is read faithfully, Sloppy is its hero. It is Sloppy who sees the villain at his dirty work. It is Sloppy who apprehends him. It is Sloppy who despatches him to his rightful fate. And it is Sloppy who conducts the truest romance, spotting, in her nest tangled with honest toil and thankless care, the lame bird Jenny Wren, whose obscurity in the eyes of the careless world is, for Sloppy, a stunning magnificence, her long, thick shining hair as rare to him and as gently to be treasured as her firmness and energy in the face of hardship. It is Sloppy who sees this injured being and is moved to nurture her to life.

Sloppy's name derives from our society's contempt for bodies, because there is nothing to warrant it but that Sloppy's body is brought to bear on the fate of every character in the novel. When we first meet him, he is standing in Mrs Higden's little house, turning the mangle for her as he does without tire. And when he is posted to observe the villain in his lair, Sloppy watches night after night without sleep, at last carrying him to his deserved punishment. It is a physical heroism, Sloppy's.

And a literal one. The villain, when Sloppy apprehends him, is consigned to a scavenger's cart with all of the other refuse of the age.

And a taciturn one. Sloppy does not talk much. But he reads well, and in an array of accents and tones. Mrs. Higden says how thankful she is to him for his reading the newspaper to her when she likes.

Can there be any doubt that Sloppy is autistic? Or that he would be if he were abroad today?

His dogged commitment to the mangle, his unerring observation of the conspirator, his reliability in carrying out the appropriate punishment, his immunity to conventional standards of beauty and intense appreciation of the colour and volume of Jenny's hair – how many of these attributes, which Dickens understood enough to write as a counterpoint to the more conventional heroism of other characters, how many of these attributes would today be stifled under the abstract label of 'autism,' to be worked upon, compensated for, and brought on in strategic ways? How many of these components of a kind of heroism that we scarcely look for anymore, how many of these would find no avenue today on which to go forth into the world and flourish and console?

Because they do console. Or they would if we would let them.

The most marked of Sloppy's character traits is his loyalty, his cleaving to the people and places and things of his world; this steadfastness is a major plot device in Dickens' novel. It is a rare virtue in our society, in which people and places and things are half-delusion and almost wholly exchangeable, but it is in the nature of all Sloppy's autistic kind, who have an extraordinary ability to hone-in on people and places and things, to imprint themselves on people and places and things and to be imprinted by them, to love them like we hardly do, and never ever to forget.

From where does this unsung heroism derive? To what are our children with autism attuned that they are capable of such faithfulness, the most noble human quality of them all? The answer brings us to that which Autistic Society Disorder is most detrimental to, that which its institutions of education, health and care would label and conceptualise and signal to its demise, that which our social strategies would obscure and our great quest to find ourselves, deny: the *singular* nature of people and places and things.

To Sloppy, there is nobody like Mrs. Higden. Because no prospect, even of the Boffins' generous hearth, can overshadow what, for Sloppy, is Mrs. Higden's great glory – her Mrs. Higdenness. It is this orientation to the singular that 'blinds' our children with autism to the generalities that constitute the minds that they cannot see: the tendencies, the orientations, the expectations, the anticipations…all of those theoretical modes that, for us, make other people predictable, understandable, and fundamentally exchangeable. For those with autism, we are not individual selves, constellations of generic content, but singular beings, to be subsumed under no category and interpreted with no theory. For those with autism, we are not social problems to be dealt with, cyphers of abstractions and hardly salient at all, but particular people to have immediately and to hold close.

Joseph has no idea what a mother is. Or a father. Or a brother. We, his parents and sibling, do not participate for him in some general grouping. We are, even still, simply 'Mama' and 'Dad' and 'Patrick.' Are we less to him because he does not subsume us under a general category, because he cannot 'identify' us? And because he cannot acquire the appropriate strategies for relating to us, strategies learnt unwittingly by other children so that they demand things of their parents and fight with their siblings?

On the contrary, we will never be so deeply appreciated for who we are – never so fulsomely understood – as we are by Joseph, who knows us by heart, who recognises and responds to the smallest change in our voice, our gait, our dress, our habits. Only with Joseph are we not cut through by the identities and the strategies that make our being in the world with one another into a sad delusion, not really real at all.

It follows of course that children with autism are themselves singular beings. Unconstrained – insofar as we let them be – by the states of mind with which we cramp our children's style and the social skills with which we distance them from the world and one another. In fact, these surprising small people perform a quite startling singularity. They are – and you may be sure they will be – their own person. Naturally, this will to singularity is frustrated a thousand times by our autistic society, which determines that we humans are theoretical beings with strategic relations, to be neatly rounded off and managed if we have edges; children with a diagnosis of autism are often distressed or disengaged. Yet, despite the frustration and the ennui, they continue to evince an idiosyncrasy that our society can neither theorize nor strategize and so cannot capture at all.

During Joseph's first year there, his school organised an 'Odd Socks Day.' *Come to school wearing your odd socks*, the poster encouraged, *to celebrate what makes us all unique.* A more succinct summary there could not be, of our institutions' assault upon singularity with their theories and their strategies, the idiosyncratic reduced to the so-called 'unique,' complete with its own costume design. *Odd Socks.* The most lowly of garments, worn where few can see them, tweaked in colour and pattern, not even in form: idiosyncrasy consigned to the easily assimilable margins of fun oddity, to be put on and pulled off by anyone at will.

What is wrong with these institutions? What is wrong with us, who allow them to ride roughshod over people and places and things. Don't they understand – don't we understand – that the glorious singularity of so many of those children who we carelessly brandish as 'special needs' – that this singularity cannot be assumed, cannot be represented, cannot be championed, cannot be *included*. It can only be allowed to be, in all its irregularity, its unpredictability, its oddity, its sloppiness. LET IT BE. LET THEM BE.

How ironic that, even had we wished to support the school's assault on idiosyncrasy, even had we submitted to their Odd Socks outrage, we could not easily have done so. Joseph would have cried out against odd socks. His peace would have been disturbed by such careless, out-of-the-blue strategizing. He went to school that day in matching school socks – the only child not unique enough to play ball, not special enough to fit in.

The word idiot has lived a number of lives, few of them respectable. But its Greek origin is a noble one, deriving from 'idios,' meaning 'of one's own.' Not on one's own. Of one's own. Singular.

That you are now on your own if you are idiosyncratic implies more of the society in which you find yourself than it does of you – it is the society that is selfish, not you; the society that is disordered, not you; the society that is autistic, not you.

*

While I am at the supermarket check-out, Joseph sits on one of two chairs, next to a plastic receptacle into which shoppers can donate a supermarket token to their choice of charity. On one occasion, the other chair was occupied by an old woman. As I placed my items to be checked through, I could see that she and Joseph were interacting. She seemed to be giving her token to him so that he could enjoy putting it into one of the slots. Unsurprisingly, their exchange was not straightforward. Joseph did not notice the woman and then did not notice the token that she held out to him. At last, I saw him reach up and put the token through one of the slots. When I came to retrieve Joseph, the woman had left. We walked out onto the street, Joseph singing as he sometimes does. We came up behind the old woman from the supermarket. And what she said was remarkable.

Not being agile, the woman was unable to turn her head, so we had to come up beside her for her to be able to speak to us. When we did, she said simply, 'I knew it was you – singing.' It was all in the tone, which was a rare one – upbraiding almost, as if she knew all of Joseph's tricks and was not going to be taken in by any of them. Chiding. But not angrily or resentfully at all. Affectionately. I thanked her for giving the token to him. 'I only had to tell him three times to put it in the box,' she said, still in that tone of mild disapproval, which is the right of those who assume the serious role of edification.

Here had been an entirely successful exchange, with no scaffolding from me and no scaffolding from the institutions – because this old woman was gloriously free of any notion that Joseph *was* anything. This is what usually makes us hesitate, turn away, or, if we engage, make exceptions, manage expectations, plunder our paltry range of strategies, apply jadedly to our drop-down list. Laden with our theories, we are blocked from seeing one another; heavy with our strategies, we are rigid in relating to one another. For the old woman, by contrast, Joseph was not a theoretical being. Talking to him did not require strategies. Yes, he was young. She did not speak to him about the state of the economy. She did not use long sentences or casual expressions. Neither did she simply chuckle and speak nonsense, as one would to a child of two. We respond implicitly to the body size and comportment, the facial expression, the tone of voice, of other beings, when we are free of theories to understand them or strategies to deal with them. We do not pose to ourselves, 'This is a five-year-old,' and so dust off our for-five-year-old style. We feel it. It is visceral. The old woman saw before her a sweet boy of five years old and was minded to give him a treat and would brook no nonsense whatsoever and, when her approaches were not responded to, simply demanded, by repeating them and insisting, that they be responded to. It was the most successful social encounter that Joseph had ever had.

I knew it was you – the old woman said, with no social skills at all, only the assurance of one who meets the world and those in it head-on, as it is and as they are. She had done what none of the grand institutions can do, what is hardly ever done in our autistic society of selves, with its blocks at every turn and its rigid formulae: she had let Joseph be Joseph. She had known – she had felt – *it was him*.

Betty Higden had to run away from Sloppy in the end, so that he would avail himself of the Boffins' offer of comfort. As she trudged the roads with a weakening step, a little basket of wool across her arm, she was enlivened by a single unfailing intention: to avoid inclusion, to be LET BE. The intention required all of Betty's watchfulness and determination. Every way she turned and at the slightest appearance of being ailing or friendless or directionless or even a little tired – of being outside the fray – the great project of inclusion was there to meet her, looking to draw her in to the charitable arrangements of the parish. For her own good, of course: the institutional capture of the virtues makes it maddeningly difficult to resist institutional approach. A remarkable thing, as Dickens observed, that a pursuing Fury has been made of the Good Samaritan.

LET ME BE is old Betty's refrain, as she expends her ebbing energies in eluding a society that would take her in its dubious embrace, shut her between its walls, administer her as it judged best and bury her as it deemed fit. And Betty prevails, coming to rest at last by a leafy brook, her small pittance to pay for her funeral sewn tightly into the seams of her dress, the details of those friends who will arrange it clutched in her failing hand. Betty died as she lived: of her own.

But not on her own. Dickens knew to write the manner of succour that we can and ought to give to one another – not the institutional kind that casts us as a problem to be solved, but the feeling kind that does not cast us at all, that allows us to be. When she happens upon Betty by the brook, Lizzy Hexham does not try to move her to a more suitable place, does not call for the attendance of officials, does not soothe Betty with platitudes: only raises Betty's head on her arm, and touches Betty's lips with brandy, and discerns through her own quiet Betty's scarcely spoken last words, and grasps through her true affection Betty's long-cherished last wishes. And when Betty asks her to, kisses her lightly on dying lips.

It is hard for us to do as Lizzy does, to let one another be without leaving one another alone. We require what our Autistic Society Disorder prevents: to finish knowing, to put aside our labels and concepts and signals, our social skills and our theories of mind, which make it all a delusion. To finish knowing – then to start feeling, the world, ourselves and one another, people and places and things. To find again the way to really care.

www.ingramcontent.com/pod-product-compliance
Lightning Source LLC
Chambersburg PA
CBHW070846310526
45793CB00012B/619